For these three people with whom I worked
at NBC from 1937 through 1941:

James Rowland Angell
John F. Royal
Miss Margaret Cuthbert

Their vision and courage gave radio
listeners much to be proud of.

listening

A Collection of Critical Articles on Radio

Albert N. Williams

THE UNIVERSITY OF DENVER PRESS · 1948

E & GL

Acknowledgment

I am grateful to the proprietors of *The Hollywood Quarterly* for permission to print the piece "Siberia: Writers at Work." For permission to reprint all the others I am indebted to the editors of *The Saturday Review of Literature* in which these columns have appeared. I am specifically grateful to Mr. Norman Cousins, Editor of *The Review*, and his associates, Miss Amy Loveman, Miss Eloise Hazard, Messrs. J. R. Cominsky and Courtlandt Canby, for their cooperation and counsel in the development of these columns in an effort to provide Radio with a serious criticism.

ANW

Sanford Ranch
Littleton, Colo.
December 6, 1947

Contents

5 • Horizons

6 • The Bookshelf

listening

1 • The Networks

American Broadcasting Company

WHEN EDWARD J. NOBLE PURCHASED THE BLUE NET-
work, now the American Broadcasting Company,
from the National Broadcasting Company in 1943,
the pig he got for his eight million dollars was considerably in the poke. As the younger son of the Radio
Corporation of America's broadcasting family, the
Blue Network seems to have always existed, in spite
of the fact that it never turned a dollar for its owners, for the simple reason that there were enough radio stations, advertisers, and comedians to warrant,
if not support, at least a skeleton of a fourth national
chain.

However, when the sale was effected, Mr. Noble,
sometime Under Secretary of Commerce, and a businessman in the best Horatio Alger tradition, looked
upon the bank statement when it was red, and undertook to make his new network not only a paying
proposition, but a brave new voice instead of the
muttering remittance man it had come to be.

The weakness of the Blue Network had always been that it was the repository of a minimum number of the big evening commercial shows which attract audiences, and possessor of none of the daytime serials which keep the American housewife in so hypnotic a grasp with consequential profits to the network.

Mr. Noble had to make a series of very quick decisions. His network was losing money at a considerable rate, and even a man who has made lots of millions out of Life Savers cannot support a whole network indefinitely.

The president of this network who was called on to carry out these decisions was Mark Woods. Mr. Woods, ex-vice president and treasurer of the National Broadcasting Company, had been put at the helm of the Blue Network by RCA chairman David Sarnoff when the system was first organized independently and put up for sale. He came along at no extra charge, bringing with him one of the firmest backgrounds in the industry. Only forty-two at the time of the transfer, he had been in the business for two decades. His background was that of business administrator and fiscal expert, rather than entertainment impresario, and thus he was subject to a minimum of hunches which seem to glowing at 4:00 A. M., but fail to come to life in the studio.

Mr. Woods decided to take advantage of the network's frailties and surrounding himself (after several false starts) with a group of men even younger than himself, laid into some of radio's oldest tradi-

4

tions with small regard for such classic taboos as "The mental age of the average listener is. . . "

The two lieutenants brought in by Mark Woods who now occupy the posts of vice president in charge of programs and vice president in charge of special events, respectively, are Adrian Samish and Robert Kintner.

Samish, at thirty-six, is a brisk individual out of New York advertising agencies, with a previous modest background of stage work. Facing the fact that there are only a few Jack Bennies, Fred Allens, and Frank Sinatras, and that none of them was an ABC property, he side-stepped the obvious temptation to bring poor carbon copies of these favorites to his microphones. Denying the jeremiads that hold that you have to have variety in each successive thirty minutes of broadcasting, he brought out a block of four dramatic shows, hand-running on Monday nights. The proposition that music lovers and non-drama fans would be bored away from the ABC stations did not dismay him, for the converse remains true. That large segment of listeners who are devoted to dramatic programs could now spend the whole of Monday evening comfortably in the arms of ABC. There are other block segments on ABC, and there will be more. It is a succession of such minor loyalties to specific interests which make major listener loyalties to specific stations, which in turn attract advertisers in satisfying numbers.

Another major programming difference apparent to ABC listeners is the absence of daytime serials.

5

As Mr. Samish put it, "There must be a large lady population in the United States which does not necessarily thrive on a diet of mayhem and disaster." In other words, out of the forty million or so adultish females in the United States, there must be some who do not listen exclusively to so-called soap operas.

To reach this group of ladies, the ABC devised its daily schedules to contain many audience participation programs, musical novelties, and personalities whose entries into a household are peppy and engaging excursions.

All of this may appear to add up to a helter-skelter of random listening, but on the other hand you will discover that it is, in many ways, an enjoyable relief from the traditional hewing to the academic pattern of broadcasting which has existed, consisting of household hints until 10:00 A. M., daytime serials until 6:00 P. M., and the nation's honored comedians and musicians until midnight. Whether or not Mr. Samish's excursions will set a completely new pattern in radio is something upon which there need be no speculation at the moment. What is self-evident is that he has been able to attract new advertisers, new personalities, and new listeners to the network. It is to be hoped that they stay and thrive with their host.

Sitting in the other corner is Robert Kintner. Mr. Kintner is also still in his thirties, and it may be a surprise to those who have long admired him as a Washington correspondent even to learn that he is in the radio business at all. His particular functions at ABC are to carry out attempts by Mr. Noble and Mr. Woods to sharpen radio's appreciation of its responsibilities, not only to the regulatory body which gives out franchises, but to the public which must tolerate it and to a large degree be guided and counseled by the various exhortations which come out of the loudspeakers.

The quickest way to generalize upon the superficial significance of bringing Mr. Kintner into the radio business is that, whereas in the past networks have sent a radio man to the nation's capital to keep a thumb on the public pulse, the ABC has brought a man from the capital to keep a steady grip on radio's pulse.

Until very recently, it was contrary to all network radio policy to sell broadcast time to a labor organization. Demands were made upon the network for free time by organizations representing both labor and management, and a balance was most carefully attempted in giving this valuable time away. Mr. Kintner has arranged matters so logically that a management group or a labor union can buy an evening half-hour even as can the proprietor of your favorite soap, to sell its point of view. In order to safeguard not only freedom of speech but a balance of opinion, the ABC makes a provision so that an organization short on funds but long on ideals can be given a certain amount of time to counter-balance the purchase of broadcast time by a wealthier organization.

Mr. Kintner also does not appreciate the traditional network abhorrence of what is called "the dramatization of controversy." If a group seeks to record sentiments for or against certain legislation most radio stations and networks will confine the presentation to speakers, feeling that a dramatization will unduly sway listeners. Mr. Kintner's attitude is that if a mass communications medium is going to make its facilities available on a public issue, it should allow its full tone, flavor, and character to be utilized. It would be a comparable situation if a magazine or newspaper publisher forbade the use of color, or pictures, or headlines in a paid political advertisement.

These random reactions to a series of visits in the ABC vice-presidentarium may, to some small extent, explain why you, as a listener, find yourself either liking or disliking the general outlook of your local ABC station.

June, 1946

Time in its flight pays no less attention to the radio business than to other affairs of men. In the eighteen months since this was first written, several changes have taken place at ABC. By and large the program pattern is the same, only more so. These programs, though, are no longer administered by Mr. Samish.

In June of this year Mr. Samish resigned to take over the presidency of Show Productions, Inc., an independent radio program production organization. Into his shoes at ABC stepped his erstwhile assistant, Mr. Charles Barry.

Mr. Barry, like his predecessor, is a young man, thirty-six years old at the time of his appointment. His debut into the big-time whirl of radio came when he was an announcer for the National Broadcasting Company's Washington outlet. He was sent on the Wilkie tour as NBC's commentator, and a few months thereafter made official network Presidential announcer.

While enjoying this high responsibility he originated the Mile O' Dimes campaign for the President's favorite charity. When the Blue network was split away from NBC, he was brought from Washington and made director of program operations. As such he was Mr. Samish's immediate assistant, which post he held, with a brief interlude as the network's Washington representative, until his selection for the vice-presidency.

The other matter which could not be predicted eighteen months ago was the emergence of ABC as one of radio's most adult counselors on general public affairs. Under the able guidance of Mr. Robert Saudek, director of public service, with, naturally, the keen appreciation and cooperation of the entire organization, the network has originated several striking forays in the area of general information. The first big splash in this direction was made when the choice evening hours were invaded on four successive nights for a single-voice reading of John

Hersey's *Hiroshima*. In terms of general programming, this frontal attack against public apathy concerning matters of national import was nothing short of heroic.

This show set a pattern which has included, in this past year, such intellectual adventures as three dramatic programs devoted to an analysis of the teaching profession, a two program investigation of slum conditions today, and series like "Child's World" and "World Security Workshop."

December, 1947

Columbia Broadcasting System

THE COLUMBIA BROADCASTING SYSTEM, THE SECOND alphabetically of the four networks, enjoys the self-created role of Tiffany among the broadcasters. Under the firm thumb of William S. Paley, its proprietor since its organization in 1927, CBS has focused its attention on *program* as a specific product rather than on *network* as an advertising medium or *radio* as a social function. The results of this particular preoccupation have been both admirable and troublesome.

The hallmark of a Columbia program is likely to be majesty of motive, alliteration, and orchestral effects that lean to the shimmery. This is particularly true of conscious efforts to celebrate an event, such as hunger, a Presidential yearning, atomic energy, or

10

even Thanksgiving. Literally and dramatically these effects are overwhelming, and, from the critic's point of view, mostly good. They are patent attempts to achieve what Dr. Frank Stanton, the president of the network, says should be the fourth of radio's objectives: "To develop the Art Form."

However, like a three-headed cow which looks wonderful without giving any more milk, this conscious illumination often makes the very messages they are commendably trying to bring to the public aloof and somewhat abstract. Like the rings in the real Tiffany's, it is good to know that they exist, but they're not very practical in Keokuk.

The above comment is not meant so much as criticism as a comparison with the other three networks and the several hundred independent stations, who see after the matter of earthiness very well.

The accent on program has been the personal interest of Mr. Paley since 1927, when he was sales manager for his family cigar company in Philadelphia. Having a young man's curiosity, he indulged in a radio program to bolster La Palina cigars, the Paley product. Sales flourished, the muse smiled at Mr. Paley, and the next thing anybody knew it was 1928, and the cigar salesman was president and part owner of United Independent Broadcasters, Inc., which he merged, a year later, with the Columbia Phonograph Broadcasting Company to form the nucleus of CBS as it now stands.

For eighteen years he presided over the flourishing business, reaching his presidential tentacles into

11

all phases of the operation, from sales to deciding how his music should sound, and if it didn't, why not. He has retired, since the war, becoming board chairman, and has turned the presidency over to Dr. Stanton. The purpose of his retirement was to allow him more time to devote to programs, and the blueprint of the organization today has the program department, which is servile to the sales department elsewhere in radio, reporting directly to him.

Dr. Stanton is the only network president who was educated specifically for that post. This does not mean that when he arrived at Ohio Wesleyan University he told the dean of freshmen that he wanted one day to operate CBS. He did, however, concentrate his studies, all the way through his Ph.D., on the psychology of mass communications. With his doctorate still fresh from the engraver's, he went to work on the research staff of Columbia eleven years ago.

The benefit of having such a man in such a post is obvious. When he wants to find out what people like, he knows how to go about it. Since he has a deep and accurate academic as well as practical knowledge of how people react to spoken words, he has a healthy respect for the dangers of huckstering, and for the absolute necessity for free and uncensored speech in our sort of government, particularly when the speech comes into your living room gratis, oblivious of illiteracy, and with all the force of sound and music backing it up.

In his mind radio has four responsibilities to the

12

people who listen to it—to inform them, to entertain them, to provide them with a platform for controversy concerning their well-being, and to develop the art form in radio. That last objective is, of course, anybody's guess, for the art in radio is the art of conversing with your neighbor. Its prime ingredients should be intelligence and respect. There is still considerable room in radio for both elements.

Directly responsible for making a program mosaic to Mr. Paley's taste is Davidson Taylor, director of programs and a vice-president. Mr. Taylor is an old-timer with CBS, having served with the company since 1933, and for all that time he has been active in the program department. He has not been a newspaperman, nor a lawyer, nor an actor, nor a writer of books—simply a radio program man, which is a rare thing in the radio business, which draws from so many fields.

Mr. Taylor has to juggle the various aspects of each program, and it requires preoccupation of the sort that wakes one at four A. M. for the purpose of wondering. As ringmaster of this vast circus, he must analyze the very strong inclinations of men of broad, yet dissimilar, backgrounds, and reconcile them. He does not operate in the accepted program-manager fashion, drawing successful formulae from his past experiences, nor does he follow his hunches. He does not trust the facile labels which have been borrowed from the world of newspapers, publishing, theater, and motion pictures to serve as yardsticks in radio. His attempts to isolate a *poetics* in this gargantuan

13

medium which slops over into pulpiteering, pamphleteering, electioneering, puppeteering, merchandising, and entertaining—depending on which way one tilts the bowl—have been back-breaking chores, and if the results are not always satisfactory, it is simply because they are too good to be true. Tiffany's again, trying to fit Iowa's third finger.

It follows that if a network has program as its core, the seed in the core must be the script department. In the case of CBS it is called the Division of Program Writing.

Mostly, the writers who wed themselves to networks do not fare well. They have been so poorly paid and held in such low esteem that only the tyros could be attracted, which was tolerable, because the network script departments have generally been set up to plug gaps in the schedule, rather than to create a program framework about which the commercial shows would be suitably draped.

In 1943, in order to guarantee that such would not be the case at CBS, in addition to raising the salaries of his writers, Mr. Paley got an editor for his editors. He braved the old chestnut that a critic is a second-rate writer, and hired, for the new post of director of program writing, Robert Landry, for eleven years previously the radio editor of *Variety*.

That bizarre weekly trade paper of the entertainment industry, for all its gaudy press-agentry, takes a very schoolmasterish tone in its departmental editorials, and has wailed consistently for the sins of the industry. None of its editors was more thoughtful

14

than Mr. Landry about the shallowness in which the heir to all that was excellent in comment, essay, and drama seemed to enjoy wallowing. He took a stern typewriter to radio for shoddiness, laziness, ineptitude, and lack of taste and polish, and pointed his finger directly to the writers as the source of this over-all inadequacy.

Neither a fiction writer, script writer, nor dramatist himself, he was a writer's writer, contributing articles to such journals as *Public Opinion Quarterly, The Reader's Digest, The Atlantic Monthly, The New Republic,* and *Esquire.* His major task at the network was not to develop the members of the department as script writers, but to develop them as writers—writers away from the keyboard as well as before it—and to indicate to them that they were cherished from above.

The results of placing a capable theorist instead of a graduated writer in charge of the script department have been discernible from several directions. His department has enjoyed a very slow turnover, which is an excellent sign that all goes well. And out of the loud speakers have come such series as "Report to the Nation," "The Man Behind the Gun," and "The Twenty-Second Letter." It is not suggested that Mr. Landry dreamed up those programs himself, but, what is more important, he cultivated his writers to the point where they could dream them up.

The reshuffling that made Dr. Stanton president has been felt all the way through the organization, and the realigned program department has not yet been completely shaken down. However, every move has been in the consistent direction of strengthening the center shaft of this merry-go-round, which, at CBS, is the program department. To Mr. Paley's way of thinking, the real reason for having presidents and vice-presidents around is so that people like advertisers and the FCC won't bother the program people when they're programming.

August, 1947.

Mutual Broadcasting System

WHAT DO YOU DO IF YOU'RE A BUNCH OF RADIO STA-tions that want to be a network?

You hire yourself a president, and tell him to get things organized, which is exactly what Mr. Edgar Kobak has been doing at the Mutual Broadcasting System since he became president in 1944.

Now, there had been a network named Mutual for ten years before Mr. Kobak's arrival, but it was a cooperative network, owned and operated by certain member stations for the purpose of exchanging programs and helping each other sell time to national advertisers. It was a network in name only, and it was run like a company picnic—everybody did everything, and there was no hired help.

It had been started in 1934 by four of the country's leading independent stations: WOR in New

York, WGN in Chicago, WLW in Cincinnati, and WXYZ in Detroit. By 1943, having democratically let anybody and everybody join it, this simple self-help device had become a cumbersome maze of 213 radio stations, and, like those company picnics which accidentally grow from an outing to a long week end, it needed a professional cook.

The difference between MBS as it had always been and MBS as it wanted to be was that in the unorganized days, the owner stations financed the operation, making up whatever deficits might arise at the end of the fiscal year and looking to share whatever profits might accrue from the sale of network time over and above the cost of keeping the outfit strung together. In 1943 the board of directors decided that they could make more money letting the network wag the stations in the manner of CBS, NBC, and ABC, and that's where we came in.

The tasks confronting a man who has just been hired to preside over such a situation include centralizing the program, sales, engineering, news, and promotional activities of the organization, and building them into a working mechanism which can be sold as an integrated advertising medium.

In the two years since Edgar Kobak came to Mutual's glittering offices high about New York's garment center, the number of Mutual stations has increased to the astounding figure of 315, and he has finally managed to line up a consistently deliverable national network where before advertisers were either forced to take a number of one-lung stations that

17

nobody else wanted, or allowed to buy only certain cream stations, leaving the other stations in quite a financial and programmatic breeze.

This successful and rapid formation of a network out of a conglomerate chain of stations is sufficient testimony inside the trade to Mr. Kobak's abilities. He is the least network-president-like of the network presidents, and his particular value to Mutual is that he is not a communication specialist like Dr. Stanton of CBS, or an advertising specialist like NBC's Niles Trammel. He is a business executive who would probably have done as well for a board of directors operating a newspaper or a steamship line. He talks well. He likes to meet people. He knows his business, and he likes to sell.

Starting as an electrical engineer, he shifted into publication work with McGraw-Hill, working in the circulation, sales, and editorial departments, and, after eighteen years, became vice-president in charge of sales of all the McGraw-Hill stable of trade publications. In 1934 he joined NBC as vice-president in charge of sales. In 1938 he went with one of his own best clients—the advertising agency of Lord & Thomas. He went back to radio though, in 1942, to help set up the Blue network as a separate organization when it was divorced from NBC. It was from there that he heeded the call to Mutual.

There followed, shortly after Mr. Kobak, a few of NBC's oldest timers, around whom Mutual is slowly arranging itself. Mr. Phillips Carlin, vice-president in charge of programs, had been program

18

manager at NBC when it was both the Blue and Red networks, and then at the Blue Network. He had been in the radio business long enough to be a member of the Twenty Year Club.

The benefit of having been in the radio business for so long is that there are very few old acts that you don't know, or new acts whose success or failure you can't predict.

The major difference between Mutual's program structure and that of the other networks is due to a fundamental difference between Mr. Carlin and the men holding similar positions in those other nets. Phillips Carlin does not attempt to master-mind the entire output of the network. He has always sought to depend on contract producers from that large and vague world known as "free-lance." MBS has as slender as possible a permanent program staff, consisting of only two producers and one editor. The writing chores and directing of the shows are passed around to independent artisans, leaving most of the work around Mutual supervisory and corrective in nature, rather than actually creative.

The disadvantage of this system is the lack of consistency in writing styles, which may not be a disadvantage at all. The advantages are obvious— an independent producer normally has only one or two programs to occupy his time, and because they are his sole support, he devotes considerably more thought to them than a staff producer might if the shows were just two of his many chores.

19

Sitting alongside Mr. Carlin is another vice-president, also concerned with programs, and also an ex-NBC-ite. He is A. A. Schecter, head of Mutual's news and special events. It is in his division that Mutual has most successfully developed a distinctive program pattern of its own.

Abe Schecter has long been regarded by journalists, reporters, and broadcasters alike as one of the most sure-footed newsmen in the business. Starting as a reporter, he learned the ropes by way of INS and AP, in both of which organizations he was city editor in the New York offices. From the latter he went in 1931 to NBC, and until the war was the spark plug of their newsroom and the daemon of much of NBC's excellent world coverage in the days of Munich. Although few people realized it, Americans largely saw the world going to war through Abe's eyes.

During the war he served on General MacArthur's staff as host to news-gatherers on the radio ship which accompanied the General back up through the islands.

With the sudden cessation of hostilities, just as Abe was settling behind his new desk at Mutual, the highly trained war correspondents and military commentators became about as useful as buggy whips in Detroit. Sponsors canceled them as fast as they could locate their contracts in the files. And yet, listeners had formed the habit for seven years of listening to hot news every hour on the hour, plus a liberal sprinkling of experts throughout the evening. Listening habits, once formed, are not easily shuffled off.

Mr. Schecter dug into his chore of making peace news as interesting as war news with a vigor rarely seen outside of stock company performances of *The Front Page*. He took excellent advantage of the fact that there were two sides to every question by pitting commentators against each other. In an arena where editorial personalities command such intense loyalties that habitual listeners to one analyst rarely know the sound of another's voice, this device provides an exciting and valuable balance of opinion. In addition to this idea, which is found in an increasing number of Mutual news programs, he took to tightening the listenability of straight newscasts by putting everything on the air except the kitchen sink. In the average news roundup fifteen or twenty items can be expected. This is fine when each item is actually headline material. In Mutual's nightly roundup, as many as ninety items have been heard. In this way the sheer bulk of small things happening to people here and there makes up for the fact that none of them is news of great importance.

Some of the neatest programming of all, though, are the tailored special events of which Mr. Schecter is most proud, and justly so. For some odd reason CBS and NBC have a rule against playing transcribed programs down the line, except at early-morning times. Mutual has no such rule, and can pre-record, cut, trim, and edit its shows. They have used this technique successfully on several occasions, the most noteworthy of which were the preliminary reports from Bikini and Winston Churchill's arrival in the

United States last winter.

In the first instance, three on-the-spot pickups, a total of nearly fifty minutes of staticky and dullish comment, were tailored into a fifteen-minute record. In addition to being able to hear what was being said, listeners who might have missed the earlier pickups were able to get a clear-cut sum-up of Operation Crossroads.

The interview with Mr. Churchill was trimmed from thirty-five to fifteen minutes. This allowed reporters, knowing that their remarks would be edited, to dig down possibly blind alleys for interesting material, a chance they could never have taken if the interview were being simultaneously broadcast. Also, it enabled the editors to cut out the unpredictable bad acoustics and off-hand hemming and hawing that clutter up most such interviews.

With the interesting new developments in recording facilities, such as the portable wire recorders, this method of news-gathering can become increasingly interesting and valuable. Like tabloid cameramen, who take pictures of everything, everywhere, for later selection and high-lighting, radio news reporters will no longer have to depend on staging their news in full dress for broadcast. They can give listeners the news just as it happens, rough and noisy, and later trimmed to fit.

September, 1946

National Broadcasting Company

THE NATIONAL BROADCASTING COMPANY IS BIG, OLD, weather-beaten, and, like all American institutions of that set of natures, comfortable.

The Sears-Roebuck of Sound.

It was founded in 1926 by The Radio Corporation of America for the purpose of providing entertainment so that more people would buy the radio sets it sold. The possibility of radio broadcasting's becoming anything more than just an expensive form of sales promotion for the radio sets did not loom for some while.

The public utterance which accompanied this magnificent leap into the unchartered waters of Radio was: "The market for receiving sets in the future will be determined largely by the quality and the quantity of the programs broadcast." And along with that remark, with scarcely pause enough to let the import sink in, it was announced that the purpose of the new company would be ". . . to provide the best programs for broadcasting in the United States."

And that, of course, is precisely the sort of introspection that endears Sears-Roebuck to millions of Americans, and, in fact, endears Americans to themselves. The "best" of course, will never be reached, even if CBS's Norman Corwin finally manages an entire half hour with words all beginning with the same letter. NBC showmen knew that then, and they know it now, and they have never worried

23

too much about it. On the other hand, they do know that the word "best" means simply *bigness* and *loudness* to ninety-nine listeners out of a hundred. That's been what NBC listeners have always gotten, and it's what they'll always get.

Now, there is nothing wrong with bigness and loudness. If there were, then county fairs and conventions and church suppers and five-hundred-mile races would be as obsolete today as buggy whips. Far from being quaint, they are as much a part of our national culture as going to Heaven when we die. Until America changes, NBC will continue to merchandise the noise of people dancing, singing, laughing, and praying.

Because America likes its religion loud and strong, with a good grip on the Lord, the "National Radio Pulpit" has hammered away on NBC since 1923, two years before there was even a network. "The Catholic Hour" started in 1930 and "Religion in the News" in 1933. And consider the farmer: He likes his corn-husking contests, his peach festivals, and his Grange meetings, so since 1928 there has been a "National Farm and Home Hour" catering exclusively to the rural listener, and commanding a choice bit of broadcast time.

And the lover of music. There was, for many years, Dr. Walter Damrosch and his "Music Appreciation Hour," listened to in many of America's schools, and in 1937 the NBC Symphony was organized to make NBC's music even louder and bigger. To assemble that giant of an orchestra, the hundred

24

or so finest orchestral performers that could be begged, borrowed, or stolen from every symphony society in America were brought to New York and Maestro Arturo Toscanini imported from Italy to conduct.

Education? James Rowland Angell had barely stepped down from his high post as president of Yale University, retiring, when he was lassoed and told to set up an educational and public service division. Today, information concerning home-making, world affairs, economics, medicine—in fact every matter that could concern the adult mortal—is broadcast under the wide banner of NBC's University of the Air.

Outside of music, which just happens to be so, none of this above described broadcasting is particularly artistic. It is, however, comfortable, predictable, and honest, and just about the sort of sound that the ordinary American family would prefer to have in its living room.

At the head of NBC sits Mr. Niles Trammell. He has been with the company since 1928, assuming the presidency in 1940. A salesman first of all, he has a healthy respect for the fact that it is the sale of deodorants, cigarettes, and razor-blades that pays for the symphony concerts, the religious exhortations, and the University of the Air. Present-day criticism of commercial radio in general, of which there is much, is mostly ill-considered in his opinion, for the only alternative is some form of government-operated broadcasting, as in England. Instead of a splendid

25

symphony, the operating budget, under such manipu-
lation, would limit music to recordings, or the output of a fair Civil Service Band.

Radio's major sin in the area of commercialism,
he holds, is not the amount of advertising that is
dumped into your living room, but the nature of it.
Listeners who entertain an antipathy to singing commercials, jingles, sound-and-musical-effect ads will
heartily agree with Mr. Trammell. They will also
applaud his recent establishment, under a vice-president, of a department of Broadcast Standards and
Practices which will endeavor to work with both
listeners and advertisers to lessen the nausea among
the former and increase sales effectiveness for the
benefit of the latter.

Sitting in the co-pilot's seat is Vice-President and
General Manager Frank E. Mullen. A farm editor
and a broadcaster of farm news from the time he left
college in 1922, he joined NBC in 1927 to start the
"Farm and Home Hour." From his intimate connection with that program, he moved on to broader
assignments inside the company, and eventually to
the parent company, RCA, as head of the public relations department. He returned to NBC, to his
present post, in 1940.

As is to be expected, Mr. Mullen's view of radio
is the same as Mr. Trammell's. The general criticism
of commercialism in radio is a criticism of the way this
country works, he says, and to the constant demands
that radio deliver more information, better music,
and greater education, his answer is the same as yours

would be if somebody criticized the book you were writing in such general terms. "Information about what?" he will ask. "Define *bad* music and *good* music, and in what subject do you want more education and in what terms?"

He is, as he sounds, alert to specific suggestions, and wishes there were more of them, constructive, sympathetic, and authoritative. He points out that the theatre, where the fine and great writers are supposed to exist, customarily has more flops than hits, so why expect radio to bat a better average? After nearly a quarter of a century in the business, he hopes only that the average day passes with at least one good program to the company's credit. And that's struggling against odds as he has seen them work out. "Do the best you can" is his motto.

When it comes to actual programs, The Best They Can Do is specifically the province of Vice-President in Charge of Programs Clarence L. Menser.

Mr. Menser came to radio via the teaching of speech and drama in the Midwest, and acting and directing in summer stock. His debut in radio was as an NBC director in Chicago in 1929. His taste in the theatrical verges on the conservative and the tried-and-true, which, again, is an NBC trademark. Under his aegis no Norman Corwins have been developed, no experiments made into whatever literature radio might hold. On the other hand, among the long-time tenants of the air waves which he started on the road to fame are "The Goldbergs," "Vic and Sade," "The Story of Mary Marlin," and Irene Rich.

27

Those are all solid shows, and the matrices of the daytime serial. They bear the Menser imprint of having a story to tell and telling it with a maximum of plot pressure and a minimum of finesse. On the other hand, why not? If there were no Sears-Roebuck, many an American home would lack plumbing today. And if it weren't for NBC, as many as a million homes would be at a loss for information, education, laughter, and music.

November, 1946

The director of the Division of Program Standards and Practices mentioned in the original article was Brigadier General Ken R. Dyke. He was appointed to that post upon his retirement from active war service in the fall of 1946. On the first of August of 1947 he was appointed vice-president in charge of programs to replace Clarence Menser, resigned.

Mr. Menser's resignation came shortly after a ludicrous situation wherein he issued orders that no comedians were to make jokes in anyway concerning vice-presidents of networks. Needless to say, he came off considerably the worse for his joust with wits like Fred Allen, Bob Hope, and Henry Morgan. For this high-breasted dictum he was dubbed "Menser the Censor" by that blithe spirit of radio criticism, John Crosby, and was the object of diatribes by other critics, who accused him of sowing the seed of a fine new fascism.

Naturally, gossip has it that his retirement from

the arena of network radio was the result of that flatulent business. However, in fairness to the gentleman, it must be recorded that he had long been planning to adhere to the sunny southern climes. Having invested his gains in orange groves in the vicinity of Lake Worth, Florida, over a period of years, he betook himself thence, and now owns and operates station WEAT in addition to frowning at the aphids.

General Dyke was not new to NBC when he took over the magisterial office. After long years of successfully handling sales and sales promotion for the United States Rubber Company, Johns-Manville, and Colgate-Palmolive-Peet, he joined NBC in 1937 as director of sales promotion. Leaving the company in 1941 to enter government service, he placed his talents at the disposal of the Office of Facts and Figures and its successor, the Office of War Information, leaving that work in 1942 to join the army.

His military record with MacArthur is bespangled, and he rose from major to brigadier general, holding the post, at the time of his deactivation, of Chief of Information and Education in Occupied Japan.

Like his boss, Niles Trammell, Ken Dyke is first and foremost an advertising man. The functions of the Division of Program Standards and Practices were patently to increase the effectiveness of radio as an advertising medium and, wherever possible, to ease the instillation of advertising messages into the

29

American home. The general dogma of NBC, which Mr. Dyke will labor to sustain, was voiced by Mr. Trammell in November of 1946 when he said, at the National Association of Broadcasters convention: " . . . not only is advertising in the public interest, but it is the very expression of that interest."

December, 1947.

2 • Programs

Kiss the Breakfast off My Hands

BREAKFAST WAS OBVIOUSLY INVENTED TO PROVIDE CA-
loric intake for the body while offering the mind a
period of brief solitude in which to prepare itself for
the day's frustrations. Coffee and contemplation,
zwieback and silence, or mush and meditation seem to
provide the ideal ingredients for that morning meal.
Consequently, the very thought of millions of the
nation's householders letting their own coffee cool
and toast flatten while avidly listening to the breakfast
banter of an unseen husband and wife strikes a chill-
ing note.

This business of breakfasting in public, or crul-
ler-dunking over the airwaves, is rather a new form
of radio, but it is breaking out all over the nation in
such a rash that it will shortly be impossible to turn
on your set between six-thirty and ten of a morning
without running into a cacaphony of clattering dishes,
clinking cups, and witless small talk.

What, please, makes people want to listen to other people eat breakfast?

The most patently gastronomical of these programs, in case you've not yet encountered any of them, is called "Breakfast with Dorothy and Dick." It is the forty-five minute trans-bacon trivia of columnist Dorothy Kilgallen and her husband, theatrical producer Richard Kollmar. There is no fooling, either. The men from radio station WOR, in New York, take their microphone right into the Kollmar apartment, and park it among the breadcrumbs. Six mornings a week. In addition to "Dorothy and Dick," there are, more or less currently, "Ed and Pegeen Fitzgerald" (old-time radio entertainers), "Mr. and Mrs. Earl Wilson" (he's a night-club columnist, and theirs is a coffee session late at night but that's breakfast for some people), "The Tim Healys" (he's the adventurer and story-teller who used to amaze your children), "The Tex McCrarys" (she's Jinx Falkenburg), and, recently announced, Bea Wain, the singer, and her husband, André Baruch, the announcer. Inasmuch as this last couple intend to leaven their program with singing and music, they bill themselves as "Mr. and Mrs. Music."

Besides the chummy feedings with married couples, there are soloists like Nancy Booth Craig, Martha Deane, Adelaide Hawley, Alma Kitchell, Ilka Chase, and Maggi McNellis. Not all of these, of course, are at breakfast time, but, whatever the hour, it seems to be over the table.

Naturally, these people do not appear by themselves. Even the most loving of couples is no more bearable day after day than your uncle and aunt. So, to relieve the tedium, interesting guests are presented, grinding industriously away at food and their favorite topic. There seems to be no set pattern for the choice of these guests. Anybody who can make relevant remarks about practically anything is welcome, but for that matter, such a person is welcome anywhere.

That, of course, is the basic reason for the popularity of such programs. They do not pretend to high drama. They are merely chatty and neighborly, and bring into the lonely home that most priceless of all human relationships—companionship.

As you might expect, these pleasant and charming companions do not scrape their toast in public for nothing. They command extremely high salaries on what is called a cooperative basis. That means simply that no one advertiser uses the program exclusively. For varying sums, the celebrants of these broadcast breakfasts will mention this and that product in an apparently hit-or-miss fashion all through the meal. A witty exchange of remarks may be broken off at the nub while the host or hostess extols a new salad dressing or household cleaning fluid. One never knows precisely where the interesting discussion ends and the mercenary remarks begin. Which is exactly what the advertiser is seeking—a device whereby the listener is led to believe that the product in question is as close to the hearts of the celebrated guests as their convictions concerning taxes or politics.

33

It is ever so much more real than just any announcer's impersonally urging one to buy his product. It is Radio in the first person singular.

It is the modern version of the personal testimonial, which cluttered up the magazines of a few years back. If Mrs. Gotrocks used a certain face cream, it was automatically used by everybody who thought Mrs. Gotrocks had something they didn't have. Naturally Mrs. Gotrocks always had. Money, position, fame, or beauty. Therefore they, reading, could, in some miraculous manner, join Mrs. Gotrocks' inner circle if they but used the things she did. And Mrs. G. uses that cream every night—it says right here. (For a thousand dollars in cash, and a bottle of the cream, in case she had never heard of it before.)

Still, it doesn't explain the vagaries of the public taste, this sudden sunburst of eavesdropping on other people's breakfasts. There is nothing exciting about it. No great secrets are heralded. The couples never fight, and hardly ever make any delicious slips of the tongue. It is simply the greatest ego lifter in the world. You out in your little cottage, who have never seen even a senator up close, can hob-nob with the mighty each and every morning. Stir your coffee when they do, smile with them when hubby drops his napkin or topples over his water glass, and laugh when the visitor says something funny. They are not acting parts in a play to the world at large. They are having breakfast in your home with you.

Perhaps the success of these programs will open the eyes of radio practitioners to a dim fact that has

34

often escaped them—that intimacy is the most com-
pelling persuasion of all. Radio is not necessarily a
dramatic medium. It has no color, no depth, scenery,
nor use for the beguiling gesture. It is not the stage.
It is the living-room, or the bedroom, or the study.
It is the ear of one person magically held to the lips
of another person, hundreds of miles distant, eager to
hear his softest urgings and, because of the intimacy
of the experience, pre-willing to abide by his decisions.

How wise was the late FDR in arranging his messages to the people as "Fireside Chats," and how dull
seem the dramatic poundings and shoutings of the
cause-servers, the diplomats, and the crusaders.

Let Congress and the speech-makers, if they
would win the people to their banner, take a lesson
from the salad dressing maker:

> If you must shout and make a warning,
> do it early in the morning.
> Banners call us not to battle,
> but rather, let the teaspoon rattle,
> and if the public you would sway,
> pound upon the breakfast tray.

December, 1946

The Eagle's Brood

IN RADIO THERE ARE TWO WAYS TO GO ABOUT PLEADING
a special cause. The first, with which everyone
is wearily familiar, is to round up a galaxy of stars—

singers, comedians, actresses, orchestra leaders, etc., and then string them all together in what is called "A Special Hour (or Half Hour) Broadcast Marking the Blankth Anniversary of Something or Other." They are usually scintillating affairs, with each performer trotting out his or her pet role, song, or story, and then, as soon as the applause has died down, making a brief plea on behalf of the cause in question.

Although the motives of such programs are noble, the results are confusing. The urgency of the need is dissipated by the gaiety of the assemblage. The relationship between noted comedians, for instance, and such things as juvenile delinquency is never quite clear. The performers do not pretend to be experts on the subject. They are neither juvenile nor deliquent. They are, of course, against sin, but so is practically everybody else, and thus the point is weakened. Also, the average responsible citizen is not likely to be swayed by admonitions from Hollywood.

The alternative is to take radio's supreme capabilities for dramaturgy, sound effects, and musical compulsion, and its capacity to reach the nation and the world simultaneously, and to project a situation so as to make it vital and significant to the uninformed public.

The term "Documentary" describes this sort of journalism. It is not story-telling. It is documentation. It is collecting facts from many sources and using those facts, like the ears, the trunk, the feet, and the tail, to erect the whole elephant for the blind men. A good documentary program is the surest means we have of focusing the attention of the citizenry on a specific situation, good or bad. Such a program can be assembled relatively hastily, while the situation is critical, which is not possible with a motion picture. It can reach the entire nation with its message, again an impossibility with either a movie or a newspaper series. And it takes the problem into the American household, requiring from the citizen neither the effort of attending a theater nor of procuring a magazine or newspaper.

To take advantage of these positive factors, the Columbia Broadcasting System last fall organized a Documentary Unit within its New York production department. This division, especially set up on the orders of William Paley, reported directly to the Vice-President in charge of News and Affairs, Edward Murrow. It was given the task of preparing periodic programs on national and international affairs—any situation which would seem to merit the consideration of the American people as a whole.

When this unit and its objectives were announced, CBS made the promise that it would not relegate these programs to the marginal hours which sponsors do not want because of lack of listeners. These shows were promised for the peak listening times, at the cost of cancelled commercial programs.

The first of these documentaries was heard last fall, on the occasion of the Nuremberg hangings, Titled "The Empty Noose," it was an adequate, if not overly exciting, recreation of the problems and

37

course of democratic justice in the matter of war guilt.

The first program was apparently a sort of prologue to larger undertakings, because nothing more was heard of the unit for nearly half a year. And then, on Wednesday, March 5, from 10:00-11:00 P.M., (EST) a commercial program, "Information Please," was pushed aside, and the documentary unit addressed a nation-wide audience. The focus was on juvenile deliquency, and the program was called "The Eagle's Brood."

For once a program lived up to the promises that had been made in its behalf. No expense was spared. The best time was made available, regardless of commercial commitments, and the subject was presented in all its dirt and grime. The program had a message—an important message—and no attempt was made to sugar-coat it. In short, the people at CBS realized how important the message was, and deliberately turned all their talents to setting it forth completely.

The show was the work, almost single-handed, of Robert Lewis Shayon, who spent two months touring the country to get his material. He wrote his findings into a powerful and literate script, and produced the entire hour himself.

Mr. Shayon showed juvenile deliquency to be not an isolated characteristic of misguided adolescence, but a national ill having roots in the very ways we live, and exerting its effects far beyond the boyhood of the offenders. Chapter by chapter he laid open

38

the unhappy story of youthful gangs, of headline journalism which stimulates further offenses, of the lack of rehabilitation facilities, of the brutal and candid venality of underpaid prison officials, of the national housing shortage, of inadequate schools and teaching, and, finally, of the apathy of us all—citizens.

At the end he suggested methods of checking this cancer, methods he found evolving fitfully and sporadically here and there, unpublicized and without official backing or funds, but indicating that certain parents have already awakened to the urgency of the need.

Mr. Shayon did not attempt to put his work into the medium of verse, long the mainstay of documentary treatment both in radio and films. However, that was to the benefit of the subject, for radio is a medium, not merely a method. This was reporting at its cleanest and clearest, which pointed up the day-by-day tragedy of broadcasting where, ordinarily, artistry and honesty are not supposed to have a place in general programming.

The proof, however, that maturity and literacy do pay their way in radio lies in the fact that the audience rating for this single one hour program was 6.4, compared with the 7.8 which the previous occupant of the 10:00-10:30 P. M. time, "Hollywood Players," had managed to achieve over a long period of time. It even compares very happily with the 11.1, which "Information Please," an ancient favorite, customarily maintains in the 10:30-11:00 P. M. spot. These figures simply mean that people are interested

39

in the real world about them, and that honest, adult radio will have a healthy share of listeners.

April, 1947

The actual score made by the Documentary Unit during 1947 includes:

PRELUDE TO MOSCOW (March 9)	An evaluation of the German question from V-E Day to date.
A LONG LIFE & A MERRY ONE (April 4)	A review of medical advances in the quest toward longevity.
EXPERIMENT IN LIVING (June 6)	A report of a unique experiment in human behavior conducted at M.I.T.
SUNNY SIDE OF THE ATOM (June 30)	An exploration of the possible peacetime uses of atomic energy.
NEW LIGHT ON LINCOLN (July 26)	A report of the unsealing of the Robert Todd Lincoln papers in The Library of Congress.
WE WENT BACK (August 14)	An integration of recorded interviews gathered in a 50,-000 mile tour of the war areas.

Mr. Robert Heller, director of the unit, has this to say about the future plans of his group:

"What are we planning? An even more ambitious schedule for our second year. In mid-December a special one hour broadcast on the crisis in education, the result of a most intensive survey of a typical American town, perhaps the most unique investigation ever undertaken by a radio unit. Then, late in December, a year-end review of race and minority relations during 1947. For 1948, bigger and better subjects, but still confidential, that the public may be better startled.

"What has the year proved? That documentaries, once neglected, are now one of radio's favored babies. The public has discovered a new kind of journalism, more comprehensive and incisive than anything else in print or sound.

"That documentaries can compete with commercial programs and get equally good ratings.

That more and more people are being impelled to action, to better citizenship, as the result of specific programs with specific recommendations. We can prove this.

"That it pays to send writers and creative people hundreds of thousands of miles, as we have, to see their subjects at first hand.

"That it definitely pays to place good documentaries in prime listening time; the audience stays, and asks for more.

"That documentaries have helped radio grow up. More and more intellectuals who snubbed radio for years are now writing to tell us about the 'New' maturity they find in our documentaries."

December, 1947

41

A Ghost Is Laid

ONLY A VERY FEW OF THE TRADITIONS AND TABOOS IN radio reflect a sober and deep appreciation of the role broadcasting should and best does play in the arena of society. Most of today's rules of thumb had their genesis in the nebulous worries of network officials of an earlier day who have now gone to their just rewards in an ulcerorium. Lacking a body of policy tradition, they were forced to manufacture precedent for each new problem. Being merely mortals and suffering from the normal fore-shortened vision of humans, it is to be expected that many of the dicta issued in the early days of the industry were reactions to immediate pressures, rather than objective analyses of the long-range shifting of the social scene.

One of the most revered traditions thus set up has been to the effect that radio and the printed page are in direct and deadly competition for public attention, and that neither must in any manner or form encourage public interest or confidence in the other.

This idea, in radio, was a reaction to a preliminary stand on the part of the publishing interests. Between the birth of broadcasting, along about 1921, and the middle of the following decade, statistics showed an alarming death-rate among small-town newspapers, weekly journals, and magazines, as well as an unhealthy shrinkage in avertising lineage which the survivors were able to nail down.

42

The truth of the matter was that the migration from the farm to metropolitan areas, coupled with an increasing efficiency in the mechanics of rapid circulation which enabled big city newspapers to spread, octupus-like, in ever widening circles, wiped out the dependency on rural journals of whole masses of people. As far as advertising expenditures were concerned, more and more money was being siphoned from black-and-white space budgets into other forms of advertising, including radio, but, and just as important, packaging, counter displays, sky-writing, road-signs, etc.

Seeking an obvious whipping boy, the newspapers, and with them, the magazines, took a firm stand against mentioning the existence of radio stations in their area. In many instances papers even refused to sell space for the advertising of radio programs, taking the ostrich-like stand that perhaps if they didn't mention the matter, people with radio sets wouldn't realize that if they turned the knob, they could get music. And radio, reacting to that specific irritant, made it a firm rule never to give a plug of any sort to printed media. If an editor or correspondent were aired as a speaker, he was billed simply as John Smith, rather than as John Smith, editor of *The Big Newspaper*. Both antagonists shared the assumption that people either read or listen—never both.

As with most of these older ideas, in actual test they have proved false. The Mutual Broadcasting System has experimented vigorously in cooperative ventures with magazines, and has found that such

43

programs provide a happy integration of media especially valuable in these days when national and world issues are so very clear, and proposals vociferous. If it is a correct assumption that one of the most important responsibilities of radio to the people who enfranchise it is to bring them enlightenment and information in an easily digestible and dramatic manner, then it follows that radio should cultivate an interlocking of itself with other media as thoroughly as it can.

Newsweek, Pageant Magazine, True Story Magazine, and *The American Mercury* are four of the once-thought-to-be-competitive instruments with which Mutual has teamed up recently. In all cases the partnership is as simple and straightforward as going into business with your brother-in-law. He puts up the money and you put up the brains. In this case, the network gives its valuable time, the magazine provides the services of its writers and editorial thinkers, and both share the actual burden of production. The most clear-cut example of using this cooperative method to bring issues in the news direct to the public is *The American Mercury's* weekly show, "Meet the Press." This program, a simple and skillful adaptation of the press conference formula to radio, is the joint creation of Mr. Lawrence Spivak, editor and publisher of the *Mercury,* Miss Martha Rountree, an independent radio producer, and Mr. A. A. Schecter, Mutual's news and special events vice-president.

From the radio point of view, it is a definite

contribution to the technique of handling controversy through forums. Periods of discussion have
always been an accepted mainstay of radio programming, but until this program came along, neither
the personality of the speaker nor the device of audience participation, nor the excitement of the issue
ever sufficed to bring the statement of one man's opinion completely to life. Short or long, the mere pos-
tulation of opinion, while interesting, is not dramatic,
and is more often than not the propagation of false-
ish information and shoddy thinking. By confronting
an opinion-holding individual with four irreverent,
suspicious, and often openly hostile newsmen who
cross-examine him mercilessly, real reasons are gotten
at, true facts unearthed, and unimportant but color-
ful façades are shown to be superficial. In the end,
the listener is in a position to make his own positive
opinion. He has been shielded from oratorical persuasion and protected from gaudy semantic juggling.
The use of such a device makes radio actually the
voice in the market place, where it belongs in a free
society.

From the magazine's point of view it gives the
highly trained editorial voices a wider coinage in a
parallel medium. Editorial specialists, like doctors,
are more than mere commercial commodities. Representing the end result of democracy's every educational advantage, they are public property, and de-
serve as broad an audience as can be found for them.

Looking through the bookkeeper's eye at the
situation, the charge that the network is giving away

something that it might sell does not hold water. Financially, no magazine devoted purely to the discussion of affairs could afford such a program. Consequently, because they could never purchase the network facilities, they cannot be said to be getting favored treatment in getting the facilities for less than cost, particularly when the exploitation of the magazine's interest in the occasion is held to a minimum by the bare announcement, at the opening and close of the program, that the show is "in cooperation with the editors of *The American Mercury*." And the expense to the magazine for its share of the program warrants at least a minimum consideration. No regular advertiser can possibly complain, for on any basis even radio's greediest customers would be uninterested if credit were limited to the sedate announcement that "this daily serial is brought to you in cooperation with the research chemists of the Blank Soap Company."

July, 1946

3 • The Artisans

The Writer in the Middle

THERE HAS RECENTLY BEEN SERIOUS CONTEMPLATION
of a strike by the Radio Writers Guild. This organization, like the Dramatists Guild and the Screen
Writers Guild, is a segment of the Author's League
of America, and contains on its roster practically all
of the professional radio writers—that is, writers
whose principal and permanent source of income is
from radio.

The points of conflict between the radio networks and the Guild are beside the point of this article. They concern mainly the fact that a writer is
required to forfeit his entire equity in a literary
creation with its first sale as a radio script. The network, the advertising agency, or the advertiser—which-
ever acts as contracting agent—calmly insists on all
subsequent rights on the theory that they should be
repaid for their efforts in popularizing the material.
The author sometimes shares in any further proceeds,
but control of the material rests with the purchaser.

The idea that a soap company, for example, is in the business of selling soap rather than of developing theatrical properties seems to escape the negotiators. If advertisers were consistent, they would also demand a share of the subsequent rights of stories in magazines carrying their advertisements. Complete consistency in this odd economic theory woud also dictate that playgoers be given a share of the proceeds from a movie sale of a play on the theory that their attendance had helped popularize it.

The real difficulty, though, is artistic rather than economic. Radio material and the people who write it are not thought of in literary terms by the industry. Radio writers are considered employees, to be called in when it becomes necessary to "build" a radio show, or "prepare" a radio script. By and large, the average radio writer has accepted this attitude toward his craft. He has been painfully aware of the crass use to which his literary efforts have been put, and he has been even more painfully aware of the fact that he does not work with bookmen or men of letters, but with salesmen.

When it comes to creating slogans and putting the merits of a given product into a neat rhyme, no literary skill is required. The author becomes a salesman, and accepts the task happily for the pay it brings. But in the field of dramatic radio programs the script itself does not sell anything. It gathers to the loud-speakers across the country an audience—preferably a happy and a grateful audience. Following the presentation of the event, as in the days of the

48

medicine show, a salesman steps forward, and, while the audience is still in a good mood, exerts his charms to persuade them to buy his product. But the radio script itself does not attempt to sell the product. Therein lies the source of whatever pride a radio writer may have in himself and his work. Unfortunately for him, the industry has not yet arrived at the point, long ago reached by publishers, editors, theatrical entrepreneurs, and movie producers, where it realizes that without a good script you can never, even with the biggest orchestra, the loudest comedian, and the best technicians, have a show that will take an audience off the ground and hold it. The average advertiser and agency executive have a vast regard for an idea. They will indulge in long conferences to decide whether to present a comedy show, a romance program, or a murder mystery. But once that decision is reached, the creative process is, for all intents and purposes, turned off, and the mechanical process begins.

A writer, preferably one who has had some experience in concocting a show of the type desired, is located and assigned to the series. At best, the result is a ghost-writing task or a collaboration between the writer who is to spin the dialogue and create the character and the advertising executives who were stirred by the original vague idea. In most cases the collaboration is reasonably successful, for there are definite patterns to radio programs, and any writer who knows when the chase should start, what sort of device should be used for the denounément, or what

49

sort of understatements the hero should use to endear him to the audience, can manufacture a reasonable facsimile of excitement, suspense, or humor.

And who are these craftsmen who have learned how to stir up so plausible an hour's entertainment that if you don't follow it too carefully or think about it after you've heard it, it seems almost real? They are the writers who have finally discovered how to make a living in a very trying profession. They are the writers whose first jobs may have paid them from twenty to forty dollars per week in a small radio station. In that job they would have learned all the tricks necessary for telling a story in radio terms. They would have learned about sound effects, audience reactions, and the customary taboos in this field of entertainment. They would then have come to one of the centers of the industry—New York, Chicago, San Francisco, or Hollywood; with reasonable luck and talent, they would there have obtained a position as a writer with a network or an advertising agency.

In a network their pay would have been between fifty and seventy-five dollars a week, at first, and their chores would have included writing announcements for musical programs, preparing Sunday afternoon remarks to be fitted between the numbers sung by a choir, and composing comments urging the conservation of fats or food or some such. In an advertising agency their pay would have been about the same, and they would have inherited the chore of writing one, two, or three-minute commercial announcements, bridges between musical numbers, and thirty-second jingles.

After a year or so their apprenticeship would be complete. They would have learned all there is to learn about the mechanics of radio writing. They would possibly be earning between sixty and ninety dollars a week, and would represent a moderate investment on the part of their employer. The modesty of the investment, though, is only financial. These writers represent all that a network or an advertising agency has to offer except for a few mechanical devices. They are what the dramatist is to drama, the composer is to music, and the sculptor is to sculpture. They are authors in an industry that depends almost entirely upon authorship.

But their way of life can be compared to that of a plumber in a palace. They are required to use the back door. Their requests for money are the subject of haggling that would shame a fishwife. Their calling is deplored by the very people who make their devices a necessity. And finally, their employers, in the manner of the politest society, seem ashamed to have them seen on the premises.

The maximum wage which a staff radio writer at a network can hope for is in the neighborhood of one hundred and fifty dollars a week. Writers working on specific commercial programs, of course, command as much as six and seven hundred dollars per program for the indeterminate length of the time their services are favored. As a permanent profession and career, though, radio offers only one thing—a spring

51

board from which the lucky ones can leap into motion pictures, magazine writing, or, perhaps, save up enough money to write a novel or a play.

Writers possessing sufficient talents to be hired by the networks are not encouraged to develop these talents. There are simply no rewards to make the tortuous development worth the effort. And even if some writers have other goals than money, they are not allowed to develop their ideas. In all other fields of creative writing, an author is known to be working even when looking out of the window. In radio, though, his day is so carefully filled by the requirements on his time that each minute between nine and five must be punctuated by the number of typing sounds that would be appropriate for an accomplished stenographer. If the programs on which he is working are transferred to another city, or taken off the air, his services are terminated. The alternative of course, would be to allow him the interim time for developing, draft by draft, new programs. Likewise, when his creative abilities dry up, as they do periodically, rather than being pastured out to recharge his imaginative energies, a writer is let go.

The result is that radio writing, the core of the greatest entertainment industry in the world, is never considered a career by either the individual practitioners or by the people who might profit from the development of those careers. The writer finds the rewards too slender, even in comparison with truck driving. There is no security either by labor standards or by reason of accumulated prestige. The only unpredictable matter in the whole situation is whether the demands of radio will completely drain a writer in ten years, or twelve. Only the most hardy last fifteen.

By the time the average author is entering his prime, ready to bring to the world the accumulation of his thinking, experience, and learning, the radio writer is written out. Not for just a few months, or even for a year. He is through with writing completely, as who would not be, after turning out enough material for two or three hundred full length plays or novels.

May, 1947

Siberia: Writers at Work

AT THE END OF OCTOBER OF THIS YEAR THE FOUR NET-works finally succumbed to an admission that writers were, after all, quite important cogs in the vast wheels that whir inside the radio business. After seven months of very ornery negotiations they affixed their corporate signatures to a basic pact which not only gave the craft a set of minimum rates-of-payment more or less consonant with other wages paid in the industry, but they were actually euchered into agreeing that radio material is literary property, and that the author has more than a passing interest in such things as movie, dramatic, and foreign rights.

53

It is a great thing to have happened, not merely for the financial betterment of the writers themselves, but because it will set many broadcasting executives to musing about the actual benefits of writers to the industry. Whenever any executive has to pay the true worth of either machinery or material, he goes into a fiscal huddle with himself to make sure he is getting the most use of what he has purchased.

The next step is up to the networks, and it should be a program of development and subsidization.

The way matters now operate, the typical network attitude to free-lance script material, as well as to original material developed inside the staff, would make the average motion picture editor or publisher faint from the very knowledge of waste.

Creating a specific case, let us invade the business life of a free-lance radio writer.

He is adequately well-known and respected for a comfortable list of credits. He has a new idea. It is an idea for a new mystery series, possibly, or a dramatic series, daytime serial, or, better yet, a situation comedy.

He knows how devastatingly hungry radio is for well-shaped new fare, particularly in the arena of adult comedy. Furthermore, his record includes great success with shows of this particular nature.

He now faces two alternatives.

Having to eat, he can only continue to grind away at whatever dull assignments bring him his butter money week after week. He will try to budget the proper time to plan this new series of his, work out some story possibilities, and in general kick it around.

The other alternative is scarcely practical. It includes dropping the work he is presently doing in order to clear his mind for the task of properly thinking through the plot formulae, dialog styles, characteristics of his personae, and over-all plot framework for this new project. Being a professional writer, he fully appreciates the fact that adequate mulling and tossing will require several months' time plus several hundred pages of scribbling and testing. He knows that he faces a task not one bit less complex than blocking out a novel, a play, or a motion picture. Except in rare instances he cannot afford to take the time for the necessary preparation.

What happens, then, is this. Hoping against hope that he can market the idea very much in the rough, and shape it up while the series is progressing on the air, he squeezes enough time from his other tasks to write a hasty sample script. To accompany this sample script, he blocks out a few rough story ideas, fully knowing that the series will develop away from them once the program gets going. Fnally, he attaches a prospectus explaining just how funny, or exciting, or true-to-life the scripts will be. He is now ready to present it for sale.

Unfortunately, those to whom he is going to sell the program expect nothing short of a finished work. Too often they do not have the time even to consider giving editorial assistance. They muse at the sample script, examine the prospectus, skim through the story outlines, and accept or reject the idea mostly on the basis of the author's reputation as a writer of similar material.

If the need for a new program of this type exists, they set up an audition to hear how it comes to life. A director is summoned and told to get a platter ready as soon as possible, and all judgment is postponed until the actual hearing of the try-out.

If it could be ventilated, the writer could live in the eight-ball he now stands behind. It is that big.

No matter how capable a man he is, the director assigned to cut the audition does not have time in the week or ten days allotted to get the feel of the projected series. He may be able to meet with the writer on a sufficiently protracted basis to get a taste of the style they hope to develop together. He may even be lucky enough to be able to visualize the type of characters that will develop, and thus cast the show, or help the author cast it, quite happily.

Of course, the more help he is in this situation, the more he will be able to cross-check the author's basic character and plot relationships. Just about the time the crew is due in the recording room, if the director and author discover this rapport, the writer will be inspired to chase home for a week end and work out the second draft incorporating the new ideas turned up in the pre-recording bull sessions.

There is, unfortunately, no opportunity for this second step to take place. The show is recorded, for better or worse, and even though many of the network or agency program officials can see far into the future, the gamble is that all concerned are seeing the same things in that vague future. In the case of a writer of any professional standing whatsoever, the matter has not progressed one jot. There is nothing in the record that was not in the sample script, and his ability to write living dialog was taken for granted anyway.

No one in a network or an agency will deny that a satisfactory new program series is money in everybody's pocket. It is an investment just as much as a set of designs for next year's auto is money in young Mr. Ford's pocket.

Would Mr. Ford, or any manufacturer, expect to buy the first rough drafts of a set of working plans, fresh from the drawing board? Of course not. He would accept only the final, finished, and polished designs representing several years of planning, thinking, and just fiddling.

And the industrial designers, how do they eat during this fiddle period? Being an investment for the firm, they are retained at a reasonable salary (with royalties for the genius aspect of the work to come after the work is complete). They are not burdened down with day-by-day requests for off-hand designs for stairways, doorsills, executive bookshelves, and assorted *chráp*. They look out the window as long as necessary each day, studying the project for which they have been retained.

Perhaps the analogy is not exactly valid. Mr. Ford can always sell a new car, whereas a network can't always, or ever, for that matter, guarantee to sell the best of all possible new shows.

Very well, leave the designers looking out the windows, and consider the publisher of books.

By and large publishers have a higher regard for a farthing than anybody you'll ever meet, particularly where there is some question of an author's getting the farthing. However, if a book author in a situation comparable to our by-no-means mythical radio writer shows up, complete with a list of successful publications to his credit, all he has to do is say he has an idea for a new book. Money will be immediately forthcoming. Enough will be provided to keep him happy and well-fed on some convenient farm until the book is finished. Not merely outlined. Not first-drafted. Completely finished, commas and all.

Of course, these advance moneys come, eventually, out of the author's own royalties, but the publisher is taking the following long chances: (1) that the author won't fall dead immediately upon cashing the check; (2) that the finished book will be as good as both the author and publisher think it will be; and (3) that the book will sell enough copies after it is printed to work off at least the advance.

The publisher is taking no more chances than a network would be taking if it advanced a competent writer enough to live on for a few months, and told him to get out of town and work on a suggested series. The advance to the writer could be arranged in the same fashion—a credit against the normal fees

which the writer would get after the series com-
mences broadcasting.

The important thing, though, is to let the writer
alone. Many agencies and networks feel they are
properly subsidizing a good writer when they give
him a secure staff job. No matter how much they
lighten his load, the fact that they require him to
toss off little oddities here and there operates against
the success of the scheme. He is continually conscious of the fact that he has deadlines which will
break into his ruminations at odd times, regardless
of how tightly wrapped up he is in thinking through
will-of-the-wispish turns of the new project.

He is also painfully aware that if he has to chain
himself to a desk to earn his bread during this development period, he might just as well be doing it
for real dough, the odds being what they are in life.
Shortly, he is off on another job, and here is where we
came in.

On the other hand, our writer on the advance
contract has nothing to deter him from the full pursuit of his idea. The man who will eventually direct
the show can get to know the quirks and twists of the
characters as they develop, checking and counter-
checking the author, and offering a handy backboard
against which the writer can bounce ideas.

From time to time, for a very modest expense,
the network can run a rough cut of the show in partial development. Without having to plank out for
a full audition, orchestra and all, they can get two
or three glimpses of the idea as it grows. Finally,

after three months, say, everybody will agree that the show is ready to go, and when it hits the air, it will be on its feet, ready to be heard.

On the other side of the books is the show which was purchased on the basis of promised development during the first thirteen weeks of airing.

Several times as much money goes into it, week after week, as the writer and director frantically meet deadlines with new twists, new characters, and different plot formulae. Even if the show finally jells after thirteen weeks, it has only reached the status of the former program—just barely on its feet, at last. Any bookkeeper can tell you the difference in cost in two minutes.

And there is always the possibility, as can be seen several times a year on every network, of the original idea's vanishing completely in the process of development, and the program's being jettisoned in mid-passage. How much simpler to write off a minimum advance than to charge off eight or nine weeks' big-time productions.

Of course, the one intangible in the pot is the trust that the network has to place in the writer when it hands over the advance check. There has never been worked out a feasible way, yet, to recover advance money except by letting the writer alone until he finally delivers.

But how about the trust that must exist when the show is actually on the air—trust plus judicious prayer? There's not a contract on the books which can guarantee against a writer falling dead, shooting himself, or merely getting the silent screamies and becoming unable to be funny any more. It is much better for the period of gestation to be passed when there are no deadlines, than when even a two-day funk necessitates calling in a new writer who has probably never even heard the show.

That not uncommon situation certainly adds its share to famous last words: "Now this series is about a guy who . . ."

Winding up with: ". . . and the script has to be ready for mimeo tomorrow at nine."

December, 1947

On Acting

RADIO IS THE DIRECTOR'S MEDIUM RATHER THAN THE actor's just as symphonica is a conductor's medium rather than an instrumentalist's. To most radio actors, though—and the following remark holds true for radio writers, directors, in fact most people connected with the industry—radio still appears to be merely a broadcast version of theater.

Radio is no more theater than theater is Greek festive dance—they are successive derivatives of each other. While it can never be denied that the ideal training ground for an actor is the legitimate stage, the actor, once trained, must, like the novice pilot, resort to different manoeuvres when on the air. Acting, in the accepted definition, indicates a three dimensional simulation of personality—height, coloring, mannerism, gesture, costume, and physical appearance. Perhaps those additional accoutrements are bad training, actually, in that they lead actors to expect fuller personal validity when they are before the microphone.

Radio, in itself, is not an art. The sound of voice is not an art. The sound of music is not an art. The sound of a streetcar is not an art. Radio is only an electrical means of transmission of sound from a studio into the homes of the listeners. The art lies in the nearness to reality of the total sound, as mechanically blended inside a control room. Most artistic effort is based on the assumption that all mental instruments can act simultaneously toward a perception of truth. Only one of these instruments is employed in listening to radio—the ear. Therefore all adventures before the microphone must be submissive to the sound alone.

Radio, more than any other of the arts, requires of its citizens an intellectual totalitarianism. Any collaboration requires that one factor serve as a north star for the others. In the theater it is the simulation of living people. In films it is the God-sense of being able to oversee all. In radio, since sound can only be real in so far as it has meaning, the words themselves rather than the vibrancy of their delivery will be valid.

62

It is that nature of radio which must be understood, and the understanding will do away with much artistic unhappiness. When actors understand the microphone, they will no longer resent it, and it will not appear brutal to them. True, sound is one-dimensional, but good performances can also be one-dimensional.

Radio is the art form of intimacy. Into people's homes, not into a theater, is the ultimate direction of a radio program. Would one increase credibility in a living room with gestures, stage waits, smiles, and handkerchief gymnastics? Knowing the average American, it would seem unlikely.

As for the emotional jerkiness resulting from radio's rapid scene changes, we normally expect our musicians to be able to dive from a ponderous *largo* to a delicate *scherzo* in the course of one beat. Keener attention to acting in the future will probably demand the same mental agility from actors as it does from musicians, sound men, engineers, and directors. Radio will always demand a sacrifice of verity for effect.

It all boils down to the fact that while radio is a challenge for actors, it actually demands very little acting in the Broadway sense of the word. It demands careful and studied interpretation of the words of the script in order that the meaning of the words may be etched on the listener's mind. It demands personality rather than physical virtuosity, for radio belongs as much to the people who do not care for theatrical performances as to those who do. The shut-in, the

invalid, the isolated person wants human communication rather than the thrilling dissonance of pent-
up artistic ecstasies. For actors to resent radio is un-
necessary, and creates a temperamental disaffection
which has unfortunate results. They will not resent
it when they understand more clearly the nature of
their medium.

January, 1941

4 • Of Advertising

Slings and Arrows

PERHAPS THE TROUBLE WITH RADIO IS THE AIR THROUGH which it passes. Too much nitrogen, or oxygen, or something. Or too windy, or too cold.

The reason I make that remark, and make it seriously, is that the ether is the only thing about radio that has not been pulled apart lately, prodded, poked, measured, examined, and catechized by the critics of the industry.

The volume and vigor of radio criticism in America has been growing practically daily until the industry now stands in the position of being guilty until proved innocent.

Most of the turmoil concerns what is called "commercialism" in the programs—a semantic catch-all if there ever was one. From a constructive point of view the diagnosis that radio is guilty of advertising excesses is of no more use than a clinical report that a suffering patient seems to be indisposed because of sickness.

In rare cases the accusing fingers single out specific examples, such as a station which broadcast, during a hundred-and-thirty-three-hour week, 2,215 commercial announcements, or an average of 16.7 spots per hour. Now, at that rate, even the most resigned set-owner, the most uncritical listener, would tend to rebel. However, such isolated examples contribute nothing to the case for radio's general inadequacies, any more than one speech by Bilbo marked the entire republic as a wasteland in modern society.

What the critics fail to recognize, or admit, is that radio is suffering no more than the entire world of press, publications, motion pictures, and billboards from inept advertising.

Musical jingles should definitely not be listened to as far as most of us are concerned, but it is contrary to most of our happy traditions to suggest that they be excluded by regulation, codification, or resolution. The way to eliminate such tripish trivia from your radio is to turn off the machine. Or, if you would get to the ill at its source, go back of the broadcasters to the advertising agencies, and still back of them to the advertisers themselves, with a statement to the effect that: "We have a need, to a certain degree, for products such as you advertise. But the mere rhyming of its qualities and characteristics does not make our need for them any more acute. It merely makes us shudder in contemplation of the exhibitionisms you will think up next."

Obviously, such a tactic is not going to make an advertising agency mend its ways. However, if the

66

critical public, as a body, and organically in the form
of its ever active Committees, Commissions, and
Groups, were to aim its complaints at the actual per-
petrators, rather than the innocent and befuddled
couriers, it is possible that an awareness of the public's essential tolerance, will to take part in the economic scheme, and general long-suffering might
emerge where it is pertinent and appropriate—in the
council rooms of advertising and selling where the
aim seems to be to "git thar' fastest with the loudest." And they sin not only through the radio, but
with every device, including clowns on stilts who
block your passage on sidewalks, cute letters that
foul up your mailbox, throw-aways that clutter up
your street, and canvassers who invade your privacy.

The problems of self-discipline, regulation, and
introspective admonition have preoccupied adminis-
trators and executives since the dawn of organized
religion. Radio has three such confessionals—the
National Association of Broadcasters, the Federal
Communication Commission, and the organized
public. That all three of them have failed to knit
order out of chaos is possibly due to the fact that no
single broadcaster, or group of broadcasters, has ever
looked into the dark closet of threats and correctly
analyzed the nature of the punishment, and the
right of the punisher to wield it.

Concerning the Organized Public, there is no
more powerful group in America. It can accomplish
anything, so long as it correctly identifies its target.
It can publish pamphlets, issue statements, and stage

67

rallies to its heart's content, but so long as it cudgels the poor broadcaster instead of the advertiser, it will accomplish nothing. However, a simple resolution in an annual convention of women against the product of an individual sponsor as punishment for his crass merchandising methods would bring an overnight catharsis. This bull against one advertiser would cause every other advertiser who has misused radio to have his advertising agent on the carpet the following morning. The fear of bad publicity is a stronger deterrent to unpleasant actions than the most powerful directive, injunction, or decision.

In the industry itself, the NAB has failed to take a real test of its own strength. Practically every other major professional organization has mechanisms by which it can discipline members whose activities tend to lower the prestige or integrity of the membership as a whole. But the NAB merely wrings its hands over the dangerous antics of some of its members.

Legislation being such an intriguing hobby, it is not inconceivable that certain cities and states may one day pass ordinances or laws qualifying the flavor of advertising copy which can be broadcast in their confines. It is but a short step, in Memphis, to such a pass.

Beyond that, and in the realm of speculation, is the relationship of broadcasters to the people of the United States, and their spokesman, the Federal Communications Commission.

It is a problem for a political scientist rather than a radio critic to determine the exact limits of

authority of such a commission both explicit and
implied. The one responsibility upon which all do
agree is that the Commission's powers definitely include matters of technical concern—such as prevent-
ing stations from jamming each other inadvertently,
and from slopping over into each other's listening
arena. The measurement and the stewardship of the
nation's communication facilities in the category of
tangibles were obviously the intent of Congress when
it set up the Federal Communications Commission in
1934.

But the major portion of the Communications
Act fenced with the problem of control of program
content. The Act directs the FCC to issue temporary,
three-year licenses to applicants who display the
proper financial, business, and social backgrounds,
such license enfranchising them to the exclusive use
of a radio channel, or broadcast frequency. At the
end of the three-year period, the licensee must reap-
pear to have his past performance evaluated, and on
the basis of this evaluation the license is renewed or,
theoretically, withdrawn.

Actually, once issued, licenses are practically
never revoked. By precedent, too, the FCC itself had
indicated that its proprietorship over broadcasting
is that of an uneasy well-wisher rather than that of a
tribunal aware of the crime and capable of the punishment.

This unfortunate circumstance results from a
vague concept that the air over America is public
property, and that no individual or corporation shall

ever be able to buy a portion of it, or in any way own it, and that so long as he uses it he is responsible, in some obscure way, to a set of implied rules for his conduct.

It is highly interesting speculation, and germane to the matter of criticism of the industry, to question the validity of this concept. The streets of cities cannot be owned by individuals, and yet franchises to operate bus lines and streetcar lines do not carry with them admonitions that the conductors protect every passenger's right to express a political viewpoint. The public lands of the nation have been given to railroads, which are owned, in turn, by individual investors, and yet land grants did not carry qualifications to the effect that the land will have to be returned to the people of the United States if the trains carry too many pigs, or do not play symphony music for passengers.

Although the FCC condemns what it calls "traffic in licenses," it approves the sale of radio station corporations, holding licenses, for much more money than was originally invested. Perhaps the individual frequencies, actually, are private property, and can be proved to be such in some test action seeking to define the Commission's real power to deprive an investor of his investment on the grounds of "poor" program content. What then?

Merely that the Commission is a commission, and advertisers are advertisers, and the one cannot be the soul or ego of the other. Radio programs will offend people who don't like certain kinds of programs, just as modern music offends Bach enthusiasts, and the modern dance offends conservative "balleto-manes." But no more than a Bach enthusiast would seek to have the directors of Carnegie Hall removed from their posts for the increasing occurrence of Hin-demith can listeners hope to find more pleasant hours before their receiver by blaspheming the officials of the network.

There are two, and only two alternatives—(1) turn your set off, or (2) apply your organized pressure where it will reach the root of the evil, against the advertisers themselves.

November, 1946

The Original Sin

CONTEMPLATING, IN THE HOLY SEASON, AS THIS IS BE-ing written, the general flavor of licenses and franchises given out to broadcasters, I sense a pervading odor of the doctrine of Original Sin about the industry, to which dogma both the Federal Communications Commission and the industry appear to subscribe.

It was first advanced in the early twenties when radio was invented. The Congress, hurriedly having to organize a set of standards by which one of several applicants for the same frequency could be chosen, cast about for reliable yardsticks, and finding no precedent for the misty business of sending words and music through the air, was forced to invent its own measurements for fitness to engage in this commerce.

Financial responsibility, personal integrity as attested by absence of complaint, the applicant's standing in his community, plus a relatively sense-making plan for programs seemed to be the critical factors, and to this day they are adhered to.

However, all of these factors, important as they are, left one matter unmentioned. This question, the most crucial, was the matter of *intent*. It was more or less felt that some stewardship should be set over an applicant's attitude and aims. Did he hope to enter the radio business for the purpose of doing a little good to a lot of people, and a lot of good to a few people, or only to benefit himself?

It is the question that everybody has concerning every other individual in the world. What's he up to?

Naturally, one cannot set measurements of accomplishment before the fact. What the first commissioners finally did, as a gesture to the weird demons that inhabit this shadow-world of intentions, was establish the doctrine that the air-waves can never belong to any one person or corporation. In the present-day terminology of the Federal Communications Commission, and I abstract Mr. Commissioner Durr speaking at a recent Town Hall debate, the idea is that radio is not just another breed of private enterprise, but that broadcasters are trustees for property belonging to the people of the United States.

A secondary, though more specific, thesis of this dogma has recently been advanced by the Commission

72

in connection with the proposed sales of certain radio stations. "Thou Shalt Not Traffic in Licenses" is the way it would go if the Commission thought it could get away with a Biblical tone to its briefs.

It simply means that the Commission feels that it is somehow indicative of evil intent for a license-holder to offer to sell his franchise and properties at a higher price than the bare cost of the physical plant. It studiously ignores the effort that the creation, through good programming, of good will requires, and suspects any increase in value as inherent in the franchise itself, which—according to the dogma—is like the Body of Christ, to be partaken of endlessly but never exclusively. The entire relationship between broadcasters and the Commission is cluttered with semantic and ritualistic similarities to a wealthy and formal religion based on a sense of guilt.

Had the broadcasters originally denied the stigma of this sin, they might have made an interesting case on the following grounds—that the air is no more sacred than the ground, and that a franchise to convey words through the air is by no means different from a franchise to convey cabbages over the highways, or by rail. In those instances, the same problems of private use of, and profit from, public heritage obtain. And yet it is not only permitted, it is encouraged, that corporations shall profit by the increased value of the franchises they develop in the field of public utilities and interstate trade. Railroad companies are bought and sold with the blessings of a democracy-loving government, provided only that

73

bankruptcy proceedings are not used to shelter schemers. Street-railway franchises can be marketed, steamship lines are privately owned and financially enjoyed, and airlines are notoriously active in investment markets where the only end is the increase in value through operation of the privilege of flying through the same air into which radio radiates.

It is a point of view that was never clearly tested in the early days when the ritual was first being distilled in the baffled minds of the men originally confronted with this intriguing new invention. It is too late now, perhaps, for a broadcaster to claim attention for that point of view in the courts, for unspoken laws are impossible of countervention—they are too formless and have no discernible limits.

And in addition, the broadcasters early accepted the implication that they were guilty of some obscure taint and should be required to prove themselves innocent at regular intervals. That acceptance served them in place of a conscience, and the past quarter century of broadcasting is merely the history of radio operators, network managers, and independent station owners wondering, not how useful to the public they can grow to be, but, rather, how commercial they dare be.

They indicated, from the very start, that they would not attempt to take responsibility for the quality of the output of their stations, an absolute necessity if ever they were to test the validity of the first, vague formulations of national policy. They blithely turned over to advertisers and advertising

74

agencies the program aspect of their operation. It was a candid admission that they expected to be put out of business at any time, for they made no effort to subsidize writers and performers, and to invest in the type of long-range thinking necessary to create out of the rough clay of radio a powerful and wise entertainment industry.

Radio is not, today, any of the things it was born to be. It is not operated primarily in the public interest. It is operated in the specific interest of certain patent medicine makers, soap chemists, and tobacco curers. It becomes an educational, political, and social force only after the salesmen have enjoyed their sport. Somebody has to fill up the remaining time, the hours when nobody is supposed to be listening, and Radio might as well be a News Organ and a Public Service at that time, particularly when such fare costs little or nothing to prepare.

Everybody knows the intent of a manufacturer. It is to sell as much of his product as he can. And the turning over of a selected thirty minutes of broadcast time to a manufacturer and his advertising agent without retaining the reins of constant responsibility is surely a clear clue as to the broadcaster's intention. It is to make as much money as possible.

Proprietors of the older media of mass communications, the more sober business men and thinkers in the field of journalism, long ago consigned to the ash-heap the advertising throw-away. The editors and the publishers get out their papers without the help, advice, or direction of the advertisers, and even

75

edit the advertising copy on occasion. It is traditional that the good magazines and the good newspapers, those that have survived the test of readership decade after decade, abhor even the vaguest suggestion concerning news content or feature makeup from advertisers and their agents.

Radio can rearrange its position, even at this late date, if the broadcasters care to make the effort. Nothing is ever static, although at the time of a projected change the policy of precedent seems as unalterable as scientific law. The networks and the stations—in concert, or even singly—can take back from the advertisers the duties and privileges of broadcasting. They can decide, in the light of their broader experience, demagnetized of allegiance to a particular brand of soap, what the public interest and necessity really is, and they can become experts in radio instead of advertising specialists, relegating the sale of products to the same importance that it has in journalism—the back of the book.

And then, when the people of the United States rather than the board of directors of a patent medicine company are recognized as the true audience, radio can, perhaps, take its rightful place as a private enterprise, with whom the regulatory commissions have protective and constructive, rather than merely punitive, relationships.

January, 1947.

SIR:—I have read the essay, "The Original Sin," by Albert N. Williams in the *Saturday Review of Literature* of January 18, 1947. Being one of those who, by his definition, has transgressed, I should like to plead my cause and that of others in radio broadcasting (not, I assure you, in search for absolution, but in the hope that you may find tolerance to weigh the views of the opposition).

At the outset, may I say in tribute that Mr. Williams has spoken his piece about American broadcasting with facility. But permit me to take issue with his logic.

The article has undertaken to prove, by a system of literary open-field running, that the broadcasting art in the United States is under the control of a few prosperous advertisers. In generating arguments establishing this thesis, Williams has strongly implied that advertisers consciously seek to destroy whatever of *public interest* might be offered American listeners.

This is specious and unworthy reasoning. It implies dishonor on the part of American manufacturers and, in effect, finds them guilty of some kind of oppressive collusion designed to undermine the public weal. I find it difficult to conjure visions of Proctor and Gamble executives, as an example, surveying the mass impact of radio and concluding: "This is it, boys. We will take over the medium of radio and destroy public interest. There will be a by-product value to us as well. We'll sell some soap."

Mr. Williams continues, "Everybody knows the

intent of a manufacturer. It is to sell as much of his product as he can." Few will quarrel with that proposition. Does he not, in selling as much of his product as he can, serve the public interest? I realize, of course, that those who coined the chain-reaction phrase, "in the public interest, convenience and necessity," have not been called upon to define it. They are like the artisans who make parachutes: somebody else leaps from the plane, at considerable risk, to test them. But if we are to consider the public interest, must we not weigh all the factors of social practice: fair and full employment, freedom to work in freedom, liberty to seek after one's aspirations? Are not all of these democratic principles woven into the cloth of public interest? And if such is true, is not that vague but significant interest served in our economy by the free movement of goods? For in commerce, there is prosperity. And advertising serves well the cause of commerce.

So I refute the implication that advertisers bear witness against their brethren when they employ radio or any other medium of their choice.

I view with wonder Mr. Williams' conclusion that "it [radio] is operated in the specific interest of a handful of patent medicine makers, soap chemists and tobacco curers." Certainly, upon reflection, you must recognize this as a frivolous assertion.

It gives substance to the remark of O. W. Holmes, Jr., that "the chief end of man is to frame general propositions and no general proposition is worth a damn."

78

In truth there are well over a thousand broadcasting stations in the United States (and another couple of thousand on the way). They present programs supported by the advertising of literally tens of thousands of local and regional and national advertisers, as diversified in interests and philosophies as any selected group of Americans might be. The fiction, most notably circulated by Commissioner Clifford J. Durr, of the FCC, that radio is "controlled" or, for that matter, even principally supported by a "handful of advertisers" usually refers to about fifteen or twenty large manufacturers—and in sum they represent something less than 20 per cent of radio's annual gross income. Indeed, the network programs of *all* the advertisers on *all* of our national networks account for less than 25 per cent of the income of America's radio stations.

No less curious is Mr. Williams' statement that "radio is not, today, any of the things it was born to be." Of course, I can only assume what the Williams' definition of "the things it was born to be" might be. But, by my definition (and the millions of listeners view it as an acceptable one) radio was born to be a medium of mass communication: it was born to perform in the interest of the greatest number. That the least among us should measure its worth entirely by its shortcomings, lends little support to our democratic principles of majority rule.

I challenge the flat pronouncement that "radio is not operated in the public interest." Ample evidence to the contrary can be found in radio's truly

79

astounding contribution to the war effort in mobilizing manpower and material, in selling bonds, in its unceasing and unstinted service to every facet of America's war effort. And the American people agree—according to the published research study, *The People Look at Radio* by Lazarsfeld and Field (University of North Carolina Press, 1946, $2.50), —a whacking 67 per cent of them think that radio did the best job of any of the media of mass communication in serving the public during the war. Like evidence is to be found on every hand in radio's daily participation in a thousand philanthropic causes—the Red Cross, the Community Chest, Infantile Paralysis campaigns, and the countless civic efforts to which it freely donates its time on community levels. Here again, the people of America agree—82 per cent of them consider radio's over-all service in their communities as "excellent" or "good"; indeed, better than the newspapers, the schools, the local government, or the churches.

In the many recitals of radio evils which I have heard and read during the past year, principally contributed by marginal critics of the self-styled intellectual echelon, I have found studious resistance to the self-evident logic that the broadcaster must have listeners in order to make money. This is no chicken and egg allegory. We know which comes first. To obtain an audience, he must program his station in a manner which attracts the attention and the affection of listeners: and he must be a man of sufficient good taste that he does not repel the public by tactics which operate against that public's interest. Does it seem demonstrable to you that a broadcaster would risk a career and important capital on a venture in which he was determined to destroy his entity by bad manners and poor judgment?

Radio is only twenty-five years old. This is offered in no spirit of apology but rather in well deserved recognition of its accomplishments in a brief quarter of a century. From a whisper, in less than three decades, it has become a mighty voice, participating in and influencing the lives of millions. I believe that that influence has been and is for the good of the many, though I will not deny its annoyance to the few.

As to the popular observation in certain quarters that the air waves belong to the people, I must ask this: to whom do they belong in Russia?—in England? Perhaps by this time Mr. Williams has seen the dispatch from London (New York *Times,* January 24) reciting the complaint of England's minority party that the British Broadcasting Corporation (a state-operated system) was showing preference to the left-wing speakers. It would appear, if the charges are substantiated, that in many parts of the world, the air waves do, indeed, belong to the people —the people who are in power.

For my part, I would rather entrust the stewardship of these air-waves to the thousand radio stations and the 60,000 people who are employed by them in America's free radio system. They, and only they,

81

are responsive to the will of a hundred million listeners who vote for or against their programs every day and to whom they (the broadcasters) and, yes, even their advertisers, must look each quarter hour of every day for listening and for support.

Please believe that this is offered in no provocative climate but with utter good will. I simply believe that Mr. Williams' listening habits, in the forum of the people, could be improved. I'm afraid he listens with too great concentration to the opinions of a respectable but narrow-visioned few who condemn radio as offensive to their own personal interests, conveniences, and necessities, and be damned to the public. It is high time he tuned in the people whose current affection for radio is so great that they voluntarily spend more time listening to it than in any other occupation except working and sleeping.

> A. D. Willard, Jr.
> Executive Vice-President
> NATIONAL ASSOCIATION OF
> BROADCASTERS

Being in the happy spot of possessing the last word in this matter, I feel constrained to except two of Mr. Willard's broad theses.

The radio industry, in the interests of promoting itself into the hearts of the people, has taken more and more to boasting of its contributions to the general welfare. After every community effort, the local broadcasting stations are becoming wont to issue proud communications to all concerned stating the number of broadcast hours they donated to the cause and the amount of advertising revenue they thereby lost in service to the public.

Ordinary men and women don't make public pronouncements concerning the help they have given a neighbor, or the fact that they have participated in the general responsibilities of citizenship. Doctors don't enclose little cards with their monthly bills informing their clientele of the hazardous night calls they have made, or that they have given a certain number of hours to free clinic work. With the understandable exception of announcing a contribution toward swelling the ranks of the following generation, the participation in the duties of citizenship is normally, in this country, a source of inner satisfaction rather than outward show.

Consequently, when the radio industry boasts of its noble participation in the recent war effort, there springs to mind a remark by the comedian Henry Morgan at the conclusion of a detailed commercial for Schick razors, wherein the instrument's many uses were extolled.

"What's so wonderful about that?" asked Henry of the breathless announcer. "It's supposed to, isn't it?"

Beyond that, there is Mr. Willard's concluding remark to the effect that the people are completely satisfied with radio the way it is because they voluntarily spend more time in listening to it than in any other occupation except working and sleeping. That

83

is ostrichism with a capital O. In India there are millions of people who lave themselves regularly in the befouled waters of the Ganges under the impression that it is beneficial to their health. This unfortunate practice, according to Mr. Willard's proposition, must be the right thing to do. Consider the number of people who do it.

There is, however, a sober side to Mr. Willard's argument. Advertising is, as he claims, the bulwark of the commercial way of our life, which has given America the highest standard of living of all countries in the world. No one will deny that fact.

The bargain, though, that the listeners hope to make with the advertisers is this: they are grateful for news and information concerning the goods and services offered by our manufacturers, but they resent the antics of bad taste, puerility, and crassness in their living rooms just as they would resent the placing of an advertising billboard on their front lawn.

December, 1947

A Little Child Shall Lead Them

AS YOU ARE DOUBTLESS AWARE, NOT ONLY FROM reading this column, but from general browsing through newspapers and magazines, the radio industry is currently the object of considerable recrimination for the low quality of its programming. The tenor of the complaints against radio indicates that the listeners are considering it guilty until it is proved innocent.

Further study, though, discloses this interesting fact—the more vociferous the criticism of radio, the less specific it becomes. Fewer commercials, better commercials, more waltzes, less waltzes, more educational programs, funnier programs, more programs for garden lovers, bans on beer advertising, more forums on public affairs—there appear to be as many ways to cure radio's ills as there are to cure a cold.

Consequently the network practitioners tend to take very little heed of the ordinary critical speech, report, or magazine article. And rightly so, for the complaints mostly cancel each other out, the suggested remedies are usually impractical, and the admonitions are too often of the "Orphant Annie" school—"The Goblins'll get you if you don't watch out."

But there is one discontent that can be taken completely seriously. Educators, parents, police, and civic authorities are doing more than merely muttering about the low estate of children's programs. They are casting about for some concrete action to be taken.

The most direct action that has so far been suggested is, unhappily, on the negative side, and concerns only one facet of the situation, though probably the most serious one. In several large cities police officials have suggested that the almost complete focusing of young people's programs on murder, mayhem, violence, and crime, in such shows as "Superman," "Dick Tracy," "Captain Midnight," "Tom Mix," etc., is contributing more than a little to the problems of juvenile delinquency. The villains of the pieces, although recipients of the standard come-uppance, in the meanwhile have demonstrated to listeners all the latest developments in the arts of treachery, venality, and crime. The program proprietors make haste to state that the burden of these stories is "Crime Does Not Pay," but their method is about as illogical an approach to the problem as would be the use of "The Hindu Art of Love" as the textbook in a Boy Scout lecture on morals.

I do not propose to argue with or against either disputant in this matter. Only a trained criminologist or psychologist can provide an answer. The conclusion to be drawn, however, is that if a community can be persuaded that certain programs actually impede the preservation of law and order, it has the power for action in its own hands in such means as civic action. What radio people and advertisers overlook is the ease with which zealous citizens in smaller cities could boycott local radio stations for broadcasting certain fare, and what a flood of restrictions just one boycott would generate throughout the entire country.

But beyond the arguments concerning the actual suppressibility of certain programs, there is the matter of common sense. The standard children's show, to be heard between four-thirty and six, five

afternoons a week, is a blood-and-thunder melodrama. The four major networks list twelve of them.
There are, of course, a few sporadic exceptions on
week ends, such as "Juvenile Jury" and "Quiz Kids,"
but the main emphasis of the youngsters' programs is
upon mayhem.

It is a scene out of musical comedy, this battle
of wits between advertisers and children. In one
corner are gathered the generals of industry, Men of
Distinction every one of them, bent upon capturing
every last consumer cent. Facing them is a tatter-
demalion army of moppets, innocent, happy, care-
free, clutching pennies in their grimy little hands,
and wanting only to be entertained.

But, unfortunately, they are not entertained for
their money.

And that statement is no mere generalization
or speculation from a rule book. Let's listen to what
the children, themselves, have to say:

Station WQXR in New York, owned by The
New York *Times,* broadcasts, on Saturday mornings,
a thirty-minute program called "The New York
Times Youth Forum." This program is conducted
by Miss Dorothy Gordon, a woman of rare accomplishment in the difficult field of entertaining children and working with them. Each week she brings
to the microphone six youngsters out of the public,
private, and parochial school systems in New York
City. These children, boys and girls, range in age
from ten to fourteen, and are simple, ordinary,
average small citizens. They are not chosen on the

basis of IQ, wisdom, or wit. They are simply representative youngsters. The program is a round-table discussion by these young people of events which concern the world around them.

On a recent Saturday the topic "What Is Radio's Influence on Youth?" was the subject of argument. The interesting discoveries were (1) with the exception of the youngest participant, the children simply didn't care for blood-and-thunder shows, and, (2) they definitely liked certain programs that are usually considered to be "adult" programs, and only wished such programs could be broadcast at times more suitable to them.

But here are the children themselves:

QUESTION: Do you think radio influences youth?

Jane Di Stasi, age 12: "Yes, I do. I think it has a very great influence on youth. I think that was shown in Europe when Hitler used his radio to turn his youth against us. I think we all listen to the radio and get very many ideas from it."

QUESTION: Do you think radio programs for children, in general, are bad?

Edward Raffaele, age 13: "Most of these programs, murder, give the perfect crime, and some people that are a little weak in the mind grasp it and then try and do what other criminals have done."

And further on, discussing the same thesis, Edward elaborated:

"If you've got murder on your brain it's fun to listen to these programs, but you might grow up to be a juvenile delinquent."

Constance Chalfin, age 14: "I wouldn't say that they are bad, altogether bad. They have programs like 'Exploring the Unknown' and you probably get more information from that than from reading a book."

Mark Epstein, age 11: "I don't listen to the radio too much any more because the commercials have gotten so thick they've gotten me disgusted, so I only listen when I've got nothing else to do."

Further examination of what young Master Epstein meant when he voiced an opinion shared by many older and more experienced, though not particularly wiser, listeners brought this: "They have so many commercials during a program that after a while they get to be nerve-wracking."

QUESTION: What are your favorite programs?

Constance Chalfin: " 'Exploring the Unknown.' "

Mark Epstein, still 11: " 'Maisie,' 'Exploring the Unknown,' 'The Cavalcade of America.' "

Ellen Miles, age 10: " 'Dick Tracy,' 'Terry and the Pirates,' 'Sky King,' 'Jack Armstrong,' and 'Tennessee Jed.' They all come one right after another, and they don't affect me in my sleep."

Miss Miles, the advertising faternity should present you with a shiny, new dime. You gave them, in that remark, a defense against the multitude of critics who say that radio is failing in its responsibilities. To the contrary, American radio is in fine shape. It doesn't give the children nightmares.

89

In the final analysis, then—going to the children themselves for the answer—it appears that radio, as usual, is guilty of crimes of omission rather than commission. The programs we give our children are not specifically bad, except for people who are "weak in the mind," and besides, they don't actually make a person neurotic. But they're not what the children want.

It goes back to the fundamental fallacy that many advertisers entertain. They forget that children are human beings. In the adult field, radio provides variety. There are comedy programs for adults who like comedy. Music, news, information, serious drama, sermons, lectures, and so forth—a well-rounded menu. But they bulk all children under one heading and look no further into the situation. Melodrama serials are the simplest of all programs to prepare. They require no imagination, only an ingenious mind. There's no use attempting a better program, because there's no competition. Kids have to listen to what's on, or nothing.

Now these radio and advertising experts will tell you, over a cocktail, that the mental age of listeners is twelve. They say it with resignation, while they should say it with glowing pride. If that statement is actually true—and they have charts and graphs purporting to prove it—the American listener has managed to creep up to that level in spite of radio's attempt to keep him at the mental age of seven or eight. It is testimony to the inventiveness and self-reliance of our young people that they manage to have any mental age at all after exposure to children's radio programs. I don't think these programs will actually make our children grow up to be juvenile delinquents, except when they have, as Edward Raffaele put it, "murder on the brain." However, there is every possibility that they will grow up to be magazine readers, which will hit radio advertisers where it hurts.

February, 1947

Sir: I am the author of "Tennessee Jed" and I would like to go on record as agreeing with you 90 per cent in your article, "A Little Child Shall Lead Them." But it is a bit disappointing to find "Tennessee Jed" bracketed with the other serials in the blood-and-thunder school.

A few months ago my sponsors agreed to try it my way (which is nearer your way) for a while. To date the reaction has been indeed pleasant. We have even had complimentary letters from college professors. We are trying to give "Tennessee Jed" an historical authenticity. It is set in the 1870's and deals with the building of the West. Among the characters introduced have been Walt Whitman, surprisingly enough with dialog adapted from *Leaves of Grass,* Mark Twain, Ulysses S. Grant and his daughter, Nelly. Another of our characters has been an old school tragedian, a combination of Sol Smith and Junius Booth, which has given us opportunity to bring in the theater of that day and introduce lines from Shakespeare's plays.

91

I admit we still have a deal of blood-letting, but I'm sure you agree that children crave it just as much as do adults. And I can't help thinking that while a great majority of America's children are at home satisfying this primal urge at the radio, the true juvenile delinquents are outdoors getting in their best work. Just think, if they'd stay home and listen to the radio, we wouldn't have any juvenile crime whatsoever.

I disagree with your statement that there's no need for a better program because there's no competition. At least there is competition among ourselves. And with the acme of blood-and-thunder having been reached, we're having to go the other direction, but fast, to find a way to entertain the kids and their fathers, for as many adults listen to juvenile shows as kids to adult programs.

You say there is no variety. We've managed to squeeze poetry, history, gunfire, humor, philosophy, and galloping horses all in one twelve-minute episode. I think that requires imagination.

TOM TAGGART

A good letter from a thoughtful man and a radio writer of fine proportions. Just to keep the accounts straight, I did not lump the program, "Tennessee Jed," with all the other blood-and-thunder shows. Young Mistress Miles performed that criticism-by-implication. However, I feel positive that the young lady lumped them together because of the time sequence rather than for content similarity.

To be quite frank, I used to listen to this particular show from time to time, and have found it very engaging and not in the least pulpy. However, of recent months the script appears to have taken a turn for the worse. The interesting characters did not gang around so frequently, and in place of the amiable authentic dialogue, a schoolboy cowboy style began to make itself felt.

Upon investigation I discovered that Mr. Taggart had severed his relationship with the program a few months after the original article and his letter were written.

At that time the program enjoyed the second highest rating of all children's serials. Only the indestructible "Tom Mix" enjoyed wider popularity, a fact not surprising when one realizes that the character of Tom Mix is a movie perennial, active in the comic strips and books, and the trademark appearing on several items popular in rural stores. The consistency with which the average child is confronted by the name T. M. outside his radio experience serves constantly to refresh his interest in the radio serial, thereby contributing no little to its audience-gathering capacities.

The fact that a character created specifically for radio, as was T. Jed, without the benefit of any supplementary promotion, could gather to his bosom an audience second in size to that adhering to T. Mix is testament to the program's general excellence.

The facts appear to be that the advertising agency concerned with the program was jealous of

93

the higher rating enjoyed by "Tom Mix," and attempted, by a closer imitation, to climb that last remaining rung of the ladder.

The historical background was dispensed with and the mature dialog jettisoned. Also abandoned were the dynamics of the appearance in script sequences of significant men and women out of the vivid pageant of the settling of our western frontier. One of the most exciting characters of all, General Grant, was the subject of long soul searching for the reason that the client sold his goods in the South, and the agency hesitated to affront the sensibilities of young southerners.

At any rate, the changes were made. Mr. Taggart asked for his release from the writing assignment, and within several months the program had fallen to last place in popularity.

Inasmuch as it was no longer selling the client's goods, north or south, the program was canceled early in November.

Undoubtedly, every reader of this book can summon up a more apt quotation, but there comes to my mind a fragment from one of the proverbs which has always seemed to refer to the radio business, but never with such pertinency as in this instance: "The prosperity of fools shall destroy them."

December, 1947

The Children Again

EARLY IN MAY OF THIS YEAR THE ANNUAL INSTITUTE
for Education by Radio was held by Ohio State
University at Columbus, Ohio.

This affair, originally concerned only with the
academic aspects of radio as an educational medium,
both in school systems and for adult groups, has,
in the past few years, come to focus on radio's general
responsibilities toward moral and civic leadership,
in addition to its purely informational activities.

The conferences are attended by several hundred executives, network representatives, advertising
agency men, educators, and journalists. Outside of
a series of awards and commendations, the entire
affair is unofficial, and representation is merely a
matter of personal inclination. The resolutions and
proceedings reflect the formal attitudes of neither the
broadcasters nor the educators, but simply the private
points of view of the attending individuals.

One of the most vigorous sessions this year took
up the subject of children's programs, and included,
on its panel, such important radio officials as Edgar
Kobak, president of the Mutual network, Louis
Cowan, producer of "Quiz Kids," Olga Druce, producer of "The House of Mystery," and Dr. James
McAndrew, director of radio station WNYE of the
New York Board of Education. Presiding over the
session was Miss Dorothy Gordon, moderator of

Youth Forums for the New York *Times*. The subject of the discussion which led both the panel members and the audience off into long, tangential, and recriminatory arguments was "Is Radio Satisfying the Needs of Children?"

Several eminent child psychologists reported that children's programs, by and large, were harmless. There was no case on record, the audience was assured, where a radio program had specifically stimulated a child listener to an act of violence, mayhem, or general delinquency. This same clean bill of health was given to the industry a week later in New York at a luncheon of the Radio Executives Club. Dr. Harcourt Peppard of the Bureau of Child Guidance of the New York City Board of Education told the group that of 14,000 children examined by his bureau during the past year, not one child had a problem which could be laid to radio.

Now, I am as glad as anybody to discover that children's programs are not, as we have all feared, harmful to young listeners. However, as the discussion at Columbus brought out, there is a further problem than that of merely keeping the adventure serials harmless. There is the broader and graver problem of providing a dynamic leadership for the nation's young people by the enterprise that has captured their attention to such a degree that they spend more time before the loud-speakers than at any other occupation except sleeping.

Radio practitioners did not ask for the responsiblity of providing guidance and leadership, both civic and moral, for our young people. It befell them as the result of having developed so excellent a method of beguiling the public. The fine music, the excellent writing, all of the things that give them justifiable pride in their programs, have brought on this further responsibility. Consequently the problem of radio and young listeners, the Columbus disputants agreed, goes far beyond the specific programs which attempt to sell breakfast foods to youngsters. Children listen to adult fare as much and as intently as to child fare. Thus the broadcasters must realize that the attitudes they support, the viewpoints they foster, and the information they give have a double effect. For adults, these provide the bulk of their experiential education. Although radio might quite adequately satisfy the entertainment wants of its youthful listeners in their few personal programs, it is not necessarily, as an industry, either aware of or satisfying the needs of young people in general.

Dr. Peppard told his audience of radio executives that the critics of children's radio programs can be divided into two categories: (1) the lunatic fringe, who, having lost the cause of Prohibition and needing something to condemn, have fastened upon children's programs, (2) those who can't be bothered to find out what their children listen to or read, and who arbitrarily forbid certain radio programs merely because of their titles and subject.

Dr. Peppard appears to be as ignorant of the world about him as he accuses us professional radio critics of being in the matter of our chosen subject.

97

There is a third group of critics whom Dr. Peppard appears not to have heard, possibly because they address their audience through general cultural periodicals. They are those men and women who are aware of the tremendous dangers of false and inaccurate information, unfortunate attitudes, and general lack of democratic inspiration, not only in radio, but in all forms of journalism in the United States today. We have no complaint against this radio program or that. We agree with the medical men that the chance of any child with a normal intelligence being demoralized by an individual program is extremely slender. However, we do deplore radio's lack, and journalism's lack, and the movies' lack of consistent attempts to take more seriously their responsibility for building a better world by preparing the proper sort of citizens for it.

And how can it be done? The long debate at Columbus by the best minds in the business brought ideas, but no conclusions. And so I asked Miss Gordon to sum up her ideas on the matter after considering the results of the meeting over which she presided. They are these:

"You asked me an important question: Can programs for children be instructive as well as entertaining? Would the informational aspects obliterate the commercial interest, or must such a program be put on by the broadcasters as a sustaining public service?

"My answer is that programs for children decidedly can combine the instructive and the entertainment value, and still appeal to a large enough audience to interest the commercial sponsor.

"First, we must break down the wall that has sprung up between education and entertainment. Who decides where education begins and entertainment ends? Certainly the children do not. They will listen if they are interested. They will listen to the programs that have educational and informative purpose, if those programs meet the qualifications necessary to attract the interest of the child, which is entertainment, excitement, adventure. Entertainment is not necessarily tawdry. Excitement can be engendered by interest in the intangibles of life—art, music, literature, as well as in cheap gun-play. Adventure can also be found in the drama of the world we are living in at the moment. Surely it contains enough red blood to satisfy the heartiest imagination.

"The broadcasters have a responsibility to the public but so do the advertisers, and the parents and the educators, and the clubwomen. In their demand for action, pressure groups have failed often to recognize the merits of our system of broadcasting, and

99

have thus made children's programs unprofitable and unpopular with advertising agencies, sponsors, and broadcasters alike.

"Because of economic reasons it is impossible for a sustaining program to receive the maximum of artistic production which goes into the sponsored show. Many excellent programs have been taken off the air not for lack of quality and interest, but because of insufficient exploitation to bring them before a large enough audience. Sponsors are wary of children's shows because pressure groups have criticized, but have not cooperated. Too often they attack our system of broadcasting as the root of the evil. The word 'commercial' is anathema to them.

"We are living in a world of commerce, and children can learn a great deal about trade products and raw materials through a commercial message brought to them by an intelligent advertiser. There is untold drama in the history of consumer goods. Parents, educators, and organized clubwomen must cooperate with the industry and encourage sponsors not only to put on worthwhile programs for children, but, instead of exploiting our young people, educate them to become intelligent consumers. Advertisers are defeating their own ends in ignoring the large potential buying power of

100

the present younger generation, and neglecting to pay greater attention to developing the consumer of the future.

"Yes, programs for children can be instructive and educational as well as entertaining. There are such programs on the air today. They appeal to the interest of the child and have attracted the good will of the sponsor. Unfortunately, there are not enough of them.

"But, broadcasters and advertisers alike must recognize to a greater degree their responsibility towards the future welfare of our democracy. America must not fail to realize that its youth represents the pillars of our future society. Radio was and still is a dynamic aid in guiding the thinking of the children of Germany, Japan, and Russia. Radio in America must exercise its power to bring to our children the knowledge of what America stands for, its backgrounds, its conflicts, and, above all, its future aims. We may well borrow a leaf from Stalin's book, and concentrate upon our children. But we must train the future stewards of democracy. And, only in a democracy can the freedom of radio exist to its fullest extent."

June, 1947

101

Radio Programs Good and Bad

RADIO, LIKE WEATHER AND TAXES, IS EVERYBODY'S property. It comes to us whether we will it or not, and what with having to be familiar with the latest jokes in order to understand your offspring, and having to base most dinner-table conversation on the attitudes of some commentator or other, it has crept into our lives with a determination which should never be unestimated.

And, as with weather and taxes, there is very little that can be done with radio. There are plenty of prophets and critics on the sidelines offering advice and suggestions, but good or bad, radio keeps right on rolling along.

Unlike weather and taxes, however, radio has more than a merely utilitarian side to it. It possesses something of an artistic entity, and this brings the normal, literate, sensitive listener often to this point: "I'll admit that radio is a part of my life, but why does it have to be a bad part?"

The many critics despise the bad, but none of them seems to be able to make concrete, chapter-verse-line suggestions on how it might be improved.

One would think that the industry would attempt some sort of systematized soul-searching in order to discover precisely where the difference lies between good and bad—some long-range self-analysis, not of intentions, but of performances. Unfortunately, except in rare and unintegrated instances,

102

the necessity of such a self-study has never made itself seem urgent to the radio practitioners.

Bearding them with that statement, you will be barraged with heavy documents purporting to be the results of surveys made among listeners. There are several such surveys, being revised constantly, all for the purpose of enabling a station operator to discover whether or not, at a given time, the average listener prefers his station to that of his competitor.

Unhappily, those surveys undertake to answer only one question—to what station are you tuned in now? Or were last night?

The station owner, if he is able to prove to an advertiser that twice as many people tuned to his station as to his competitor's, can thereby claim to be the ideal choice of an advertising medium. And thus the surveys are gotten together. Phone calls are made, personal visits arranged, and elaborate charts and graphs erected showing the disposition, at all hours of the day, of all listening.

These surveys consider, naturally, only the disposition of homes where the radio is turned on. The figures then handed out to the advertisers and the public indicate what percentage of the available (sets turned on) listeners are listening to a specific station or program.

The custom of following such a survey too closely, or at all, for that matter, presents the same danger as having your small son criticize your auto-driving ability. He enjoys going for a ride so much that he does not analyze the goodness or badness of the driving. Questioning on the basis of sets in use ignores the fundamental problem to be faced. If you are listening, *why* are you listening, and if you are not, *why not?*

Most people turn on their radios the way they open a window upon entering a closed room. It is a matter of habit and custom. And they like company, even if it be disembodied, the way they like fresh air. It gives them a sense of existence.

They do not, though, always listen, any more than they conscientiously breathe. There is a difference between listening and hearing, and for all the surveys, studies, graphs, and charts, the self-analysts fail to face that crucial question: If your radio is on, are you listening to it, or merely hearing it?

Shortly before the war one effort was made to get more deeply into the matter. A shrewd individual named Horace Schwerin, in cooperation with Frank Stanton, then director of research at Columbia Broadcasting System, and now president of that colossus, developed a device which measured your palpitations as you listened to a radio show. A set of switches was installed in the listener's hand and connected to a machine. By merely pressing one of two buttons, the listener could indicate like or dislike. Lack of interest was recorded by sheer normality on the chart. Interest made the resultant chart show little mountains. An interesting thing about this device was that it could be simultantously attached to a number of people, giving a composite picture of the likes and dislikes of an audience made up of a cross-section of an average public.

Again, there was one great flaw in that reasoning, although it advanced self-analysis another step. The machine simply records the existence of bad and good, but is unable to supply any facts or figures toward the determination of why a certain instant of a program is more acceptable than another. They still do not grapple with the thing of most importance: How can we make the good permanent and the bad become good?

It is possibly because of the complexity of the system. There are programs on the air which everybody knows are bad. Why do they continue? Bad writing, inept acting, illiterate handling of a matter of great interest, or just sheer pedestrianism. We do not speak of goodness and badness in moral terms, but only as we would if a book, claiming our attention because of the name of the author or the nobility of the subject, should turn out to be misspelled, poorly printed, and scatter-brained in its conception.

Why? There are a thousand rationalizations. "I know this program, for which I am responsible, is bad. But people seem to like it." "This may be bad, but I've heard worse." "Bad? The audience in the studio loved it." Etc., etc., etc.

People look and hear, but they do not necessarily watch and listen. The poorness of one show should not justify more poorness. When a radio proprietor feels those occasional twinges of awareness of cheapness, it is the time to make immediate, even if small, revisions. It is no time to wait and

105

see if the charts show any trends from mere badness to audience disgust. They won't. Again, like the weather, everybody talks about it, but nobody does anything about it.

However, you can, if you desire, do this: You can stop merely hearing your radio, and listen to it. And on the basis of how you feel when you listen, make suggestions. The mail from listeners is very heavy in the radio stations, but a letter bearing a concrete suggestion is a rare thing. Especially a letter which is legible and not written with a charred stick on wrapping paper. Who knows? Once the awareness of you, out there, is felt up in the carpeted vice-president's corridor, something may happen, if nothing more than a slow elephantine glancing up at the world outside. Even that will be a concession on the part of radio to the times in which we live.

June, 1946

5 • Horizons

The Platter Business

THERE IS ONE AREA WHERE THE RADIO AND PUBLISH-
ing business roll along side by side, enjoying the
same headaches of sales and distribution, and sharing
the same slender probabilities of fortune.

It is in the field of transcribed programs that
the clover grows suspiciously like the weeds upon
which the book trade ranges.

First, though, a brief picture of the radio program business as a whole. Although the networks
and many of the larger, unaffiliated radio stations
employ a large staff of program producers, directors,
and writers, the big money is made by independent
producers. These impresarios capture the radio
rights to story material, the exclusive call on the
radio appearances of stage and screen stars, a contract to be the sole radio entrepreneur for an important musical group, or combinations of all three.
They then work up a radio program featuring their
stable of performers, and sell it for a weekly fee to

107

a commercial sponsor who broadcasts it in time he has purchased. This fee is normally several hundreds of dollars more than the producer actually pays his troupe, the difference being profit for his time, effort, imagination, and ingenuity. In these cases the advertising agency concerned with the program and the network or station presenting it have no actual finger in the pie, although they hover not too obscurely in the background.

These programs, though, are heard only on networks, sponsored by national advertisers, for the program costs in the average evening half-hour presentation rarely fall below four thousand dollars, and mount, in some cases, to fifteen and twenty thousand.

What are you hearing, then, on your local station, when your corner druggist sponsors a star-studded drama or musical comedy? The druggist is not a national advertiser. The station you hear is your own low-power local station, affiliated with no network, and you know for a fact that the thirty minutes' time costs the druggist not more than thirty dollars. How, then, can he afford a Big Time program?

He probably is a client of Frederick Ziv, Louis G. Cowan, Inc., or NBC's Radio Recording Division, the three major operators in the transcribed program field, where it might be said that they are publishers of radio programs.

Perhaps the program your duggist sponsors is "Murder at Midnight," a quite high-class, adult mystery thriller, capably written, expertly produced, and in every way as good as the chillers that wealthy national advertisers shoot down the networks to you.

Each single episode of MaM costs its producer, Louis Cowan (otherwise famous as the proprietor of "The Quiz Kids,") slightly more than two thousand dollars. And yet, week after week, your druggist is able to sponsor it for the few dollars he can afford to spend on radio advertising.

The fact is that he buys only one copy of the show for a sum which varies from five to five hundred dollars, depending upon the population reached by your local station. If the station's charge for a half hour of air time is thirty dollars, then the cost to the local sponsor will be in the neighborhood of ten dollars per week.

You quickly come to the conclusion that the producer has to sell quite a few copies of that particular program to recapture his two thousand-odd dollars. So does a publisher have to sell quite a stock of books at three dollars each to recapture his manufacturing costs. However, there are upwards of three hundred stations to whom producer Cowan can peddle copies of his show.

These stations are independent stations without other sources of program material, and network affiliates desiring to fill time when they are not serviced by their network. They are the rank and file of the radio stations in the country. There are considerably more than three hundred such stations on

the air, but transcribed programs are sold on a "protected" basis, which is to say that "Murder at Midnight" will not be sold to another station in the same
listening area. Slice the air any way you want, three
hundred buyers is the top potential with that exclu-
sivity restriction. However, with the average sale
price of such a show at fifty dollars, the producer
stands a good chance of recovering his production
costs and even making a fair profit in the long run.

It is that long run aspect of this business that
causes the headaches. In order to make an original
sale, the producer has to have at least thirty-nine and
preferaby fifty-two programs recorded—already published, as it were. No sponsor will take a chance on
a prospectus and start his series in your town with
only the promise that the rest of the series will be
forthcoming.

Thus, the producer has to capitalize his venture to the amount (in this case) of some seventy-
five thousand dollars, and not until this is all spent
can he begin to get it back at the rate of ten dollars
here, twenty there, and so on. However, like books,
once published, there the programs are. They can
be sold to a new druggist in another town ten years
hence, and to that audience the shows will be every
bit as fresh and new as they are to you tonight.
Eventually, if he lives long enough, the producer of
a transcribed series, like a publisher, will get his
money back so long as he keeps pounding the small-
town pavements in search of new druggists and similar small advertisers with an extra five or ten dollars
110

per week available for the great adventure of radio advertising.

November, 1947

F-M

IN 1935 A RADIO ENGINEER, MAJOR EDWIN H. ARM-strong, developed a new technique for transmitting sound by radio waves. Although the mechanics of this new method are not easily visualized by the non-engineer, Frequency Modulation, or FM, as it is known, presented broadcasters with a completely new means of transmission.

Only the cabinet, the speaker, and the sound amplifier units of ordinary radio sets would remain unchanged in Major Armstrong's new domain. His radios would contain completely new innards, and he posed for the broadcasting industry a set of challenges which are being squarely met only this last year, twelve years after the invention itself.

The challenges were that while FM offered radio listeners distinct advantages over the method then, and now, in use, it would out-mode and require the junking of millions of dollars' worth of receiving and transmitting equipment.

Although there are frequencies available in the United States for nearly 5,000 FM stations, there were, at the end of October of 1946, eleven years after Major Armstrong first demonstrated his invention, only sixty-six stations in operation, most of

111

them merely repeating simultaneously the programs of regular, standard stations.

To explain this amazing failure of a notoriously gadget and innovation conscious people to fall all over themselves to turn out the old and bring in the new, one must recall the classic gasoline-pill tale. As was supposed to have happened in the case of the pill which could make gasoline from plain water at a fraction of a cent per gallon, the equipment manufacturers have been accused of entering secret agreements not to make FM receivers and, consequently, to keep FM stations off the air.

It was, however, merely another case of the old free enterprise whirlpool. Radio manufacturers, always eager to make an honest dollar, have been ready to build sets when sufficient buyers turn up. Purchasers, on the other hand, have been waiting for stations to start operations before they buy receiving sets. Stations, on the third hand, have had to wait until enough sets were in an area to form a market for an advertiser in order to inveigle him to foot the bills for programs.

It took the pressure of war-savings seeking investment, plus war-trained men and women eager to invade new fields, to cut through the edge of the whirlpool. How deeply they have cut can be appreciated by the knowledge that in the first year after October, 1946, 328 FM stations went into operation in addition to those previously on the air, and the Federal Communications Commisssion has authorized nearly 700 more, which are in various stages of construction. In addition, there are some 125 more license applications waiting to be heard. It will not be many more months before FM will be a going and profitable concern, and it is possible to anticipate that within a few years the present standard broadcasting stations will become obsolete.

The present networks and stations will not, of course, be driven from the air by the newcomers, but their stations will shift to FM, and slowly the FM band on radios will become the common band in use, and the currently employed AM band (for Amplitude Modulation) will go up on the novelty shelf along with short-wave.

Most listeners are more or less aware of FM's mechanical advantages over standard broadcasting. The music lover knows that FM has a top range of 15,000 cycles, while AM mutters along at a maximum of about 6,000 cycles, to the near-ruin of music. An entire generation of music followers, having substituted the radio and the phonograph for concert-going, has never felt the dynamics of great music. It hears the tune and the beat, but has never known music's sublimity.

And then there is the matter of static. Electrical interference is to a greater or lesser degree a function of AM transmission. It is no more a part of FM than acetylene lamps are of 1947 automobiles.

Two other common sufferings of AM radio have been done away with through Major Armstrong's invention. They are fading of volume and lack of selectivity. In FM the discouraging overtones of

113

distant stations are completely eliminated, and the daytime signal is exactly as strong and predictable as the night-time signal.

Beyond these purely technical advantages, the listener will begin to sense many broader differences as he finds his favorite among the new FM stations in his locality. By its very nature the FM system of broadcasting suggests cures to several of the most irritating excesses present in commercial radio today. Of special significance to the socially conscious is the fact that FM, like television, being a high-frequency operation, is theoretically limited to an area enclosed by the horizon as seen from the tip of the antenna. This enables the licensing of nearly 5,000 stations in the country, thereby giving voice to many interesting and worthwhile organizations devoted to special interests, which could not qualify as stewards of the general public interest in the competition for the fewer available standard broadcast channels in the lower frequencies. Universities, churches, community and civic groups, labor and farm organizations—all of these can now erect their own radio stations to serve their particular local audiences without pre-empting broadcast availabilities necessary for adequate general coverage of a locality.

The high cost of construction and operation of standard broadcast facilities has heretofore contributed considerably to listener abuse. The necessity for eking an income out of every moment of broadcast time has led to the unfortunate overcrowding of the air with intermittent singing and shouting commer-

114

cials which paralyze listeners' receptivity to good programming. Being forced, by high rates, into bare
breathing spaces, advertisers have had to resort to
noise and astounding effects to claim attention for
their products. And for the same reason of under-
standably high rates, local merchants who might
otherwise perform a useful shopping service by announcing special sales, bargains, and shipments of
scarce goods have been crowded aside by the wealthier
national manufacturers of patent medicines and nos-
trums.

An FM station competently serving the community lying within its area of coverage can be operated for as little as fifteen or twenty thousand dollars
a year. These low costs immediately make it no
longer necessary for every second breath to be devoted
to advertising. The operator has a much wider mar-
gin of profit, and can serve, in fact as well as in spirit,
his community. A larger percentage of his broadcast
day can be devoted to programs of genuine community interest. And, being able to offer advertising time
for a much lower cost, the FM station can be a truly
useful information agent for both the local merchants
and the local purchasers.

But beyond the purely dollar-and-cents benefits
of lower cost radio service, there is the indisputable
fact that the greater number of FM stations will result in a stricter competition for audience. This will
bring about a more serious study of the public likes
and dislikes, and will dictate a closer adherence to audience demands. With many of our larger cities now

115

being served solely by four national network stations, set owners are at the mercy of the likes of "Listener," an individual who does not exist. College professor in the Northwest, manual laborer in Florida, married clerk in New York City, wealthy retired widow in California, "Listener" is all of these at once, and one hundred million others, and yet a single program taste is assigned to him as the result of endless averaging and normalizing.

The days of "Listener" are numbered with FM, and radio programming will expand in all directions at once. It will soon come to pass that the householder in practically every area of the country will be able to choose his radio fare from as wide a set of qualifications as he does his magazine subscription list.

Perhaps the most thoughtful analysis of the place FM will take in the scheme of our radio system was made by Mr. Mark Woods, president of the American Broadcasting Company, when he said:

"FM will be the principal medium of broadcasting, especially in urban areas. With few exceptions, every station operating on a regional or local channel can not only improve its service in the area now being served, but can extend that service materially. Eventually FM should replace all local and regional stations in urban areas so that these channels can be available for rural service at higher power."

And when will this thing come true?

"It is here now (says Mr. Edward Codel,

publisher of *FM Business,* the industry's lusty
young tradepaper) . If the set you buy today does
not include FM, you are getting a pre-war model,
because from now on out you are going to find
the bulk of your listening pleasure in FM."

July, 1947

Television

IT IS NOW A FEW WEEKS AFTER LABOR DAY, WHICH
was sort of a vague deadline after which most people
promised to find out when they could get a television
set for their home, and, moreover, what they could
expect in the way of programs.

There's just one more corner to round, which is
news, inasmuch as television has been just around the
next corner since 1936. But this is really the last
corner.

As of this month there are still only about five
thousand television sets operating in Manhattan.
There were only that many before the war, and these
sets, in fact, are the very same ones. However, within
a matter of hours, one gathers, manufacturers will
have unplugged the last bottleneck in parts manufacture, and will be turning 1946 model sets out at the
rate of forty to fifty thousand a month. Certainly by
the first of the year, at any rate.

These sets will cost you anywhere from two
hundred to two thousand dollars or so. The cheapest
RCA table models will retail for about one hundred

117

and fifty dollars, with thirty to fifty dollars more re-quired for installation. They will provide an ade-quate means for enjoying the programs, although the viewing screen is a bit small to enable a roomful of people to sit back at any distance and see the show. And that particular set will be for television only. You'll still have to keep your radio and your record player handy.

At the other end of the price range stands the Allen B. Du Mont console model retailing at more than two thousand dollars. This set, though, includes a magnificent long-short-wave radio, AM and FM, and an automatic record player that can handle ten- and twelve-inch discs intermingled. The screen is large enough to give a fine picture to people seated anywhere in a large room, and the reproductions are equally visible in a lighted room or in the dark, un-like home movies. This last fact will be a source of comfort to social scientists who feared that American housewives might develop owlish characteristics from spending their days in the shadows, entranced by hour after hour of flickering entertainment.

How far out in the suburbs can a person live and still enjoy television? Forty to fifty miles. The range of television stations is regulated by law—power of transmission and height of antenna to be adjusted so that no station, except under freakish conditions, shall spill beyond the arbitrary range.

What cities have television stations on the air now? New York, Chicago, Washington, Philadelphia, Schenectady, and Los Angeles have regular television service, and Du Mont, which operates stations in New York and Washington, has plans under way to erect stations in Pittsburgh, Cleveland, and Cincinnati. In addition to those they are building for themselves, they are acting as contractors for a station in St. Louis and a station in Detroit.

Other installations are anticipated, and the FCC has granted licenses to a number of other applicants, although it remains to be seen how many of these will actually avail themselves of their privileges. The paucity of sets in operation still dictates a stringently low-priced sale of time on television, and only extremely elaborate organizations can afford to undertake the handsome loss necessary at this point, even as experimentation.

This factor is of even greater significance outside the metropolitan centers, where a number of potentially valuable community channels are now unused. In a decade or so, when every farm can have its set, these community channels will prove to be fine investments, and will guarantee that practically every city of twenty thousand or so inhabitants, with the surrounding areas, can be served by at least one station.

Will the television stations be connected by networks? Yes, but they will not depend on simultaneous broadcasts from New York or Hollywood, all the way up and down the net, for their programming. Already a co-axial cable links New York with Washington, and the A.T.&T., which owns and operates the network facility, is planning new lines all the time.

Other means of linkage are being developed, such as high frequency relay stations at close intervals. Programs are simply bounced across the country by being received by station B from station A, and simultaneously broadcast on to station C, which in turn bounces them on to station D.

Film will play a major role in affecting the simultaneity of coverage that radio networks now achieve. Film, though, will give viewers, or whatever the term will be, several advantages over radio-broadcasting. Without depending on expensive line charges, a live talent program broadcast tonight in New York can be filmed as it is being shown, and the film sent to other stations throughout the country at different times. The implication is that the savings in line charges will be expended in bettering the shows. Also, programs can be pre-filmed in order to achieve wider distribution, and, in the pre-filming, would benefit from editing and trimming. Standard Hollywood feature films, though, will not play a substantial part in the programming. Not only are they too long for commercial use, but the motion-picture people would not allow them to be used until they had exhausted their theatrical market, in order to avoid competition. Film will be especially made for television, and several firms have recently been organized for that particular purpose.

As far as programs are concerned, the medium is much further advanced than an analyst would an-

ticipate in a situation where public outlets have been
so restricted. This is due to the fact that because so
very many things are interesting to watch, using
common sense, it is difficult to produce a bad show.
Exhibitions of all sorts, special events from fires to
fights, parades, elections, conventions, sports—this is
all fare that will lift us out of the doldrums in which
radio has becalmed us. With a world full of such a
number of things there will simply be no time for
daytime serials. Unfortunately, though, audience
participation programs, the bane of evening radio,
will possibly blossom in television. It has been bad
enough listening to people laughing at something we
could not see. The only thing worse will be to find
out what it is they are laughing at.

As might be expected, the most unpalatable of
television programs have been adaptations of other
media. The average stage play, although one might
think it would lend itself to television better than
to radio, suffers extremely from lack of funds. Producers simply cannot expect to devote four or five
thousand dollars and two or three days of rehearsing
to the creditable mounting of a play which cost thirty
thousand dollars to stage originally and took six
weeks for preparation. Most plays, for all the love
and care which is given them by extremely professional stage people, creak and groan unbearably on
television.

The medium is best geared for seeing things
happen that actually happen, rather than heavily

created unreality. Interviews, special events, and intelligently made film documentaries—such will make the best television fare.

October, 1946

Listener Councils

OFTEN, IN THE COURSE OF SOME CRITICAL COMMENT or other against the radio industry, this column has suggested that the listeners, and the listeners alone, can, in the end, actually correct shoddy or inadequate programming.

Unfortunately, we all know how futile even the most sustained barrage of letters is. In most cases suggestions are read, and even appreciated, but mere individual opinions count for very little in this world of powerful pressures. What is needed is an instrument whereby the opinions of listeners can be brought in their full weight to the appropriate and attentive authorities.

Such instruments have been partially developed in the past, on the national level. Such groups as the General Federation of Women's Clubs, the National P-T-A, the Junior League, and the National Council of Churches have radio councils which act as a liaison between their vast membership and the radio industry.

However, two weaknesses of operation on the national level defeat the ultimate attempts. For one thing, the organizations do not represent Listeners.

122

They represent listening churchgoers, listening club-women, or listening parents. As such, their primary interest is the development of other matters than a better radio system, and radio listening is only a partial means to a different end.

Also, they represent listeners on a national, rather than a local scale. Suggestions, thus, are not able to encompass the specific listening habits of the people of one community, taking into consideration civic affairs and other local interests which need integration with general listening.

What is called for is a fragmentation of listener organizations to the local level. Through a congregation of such nuclear groups, the perpetual suggestions of listeners throughout the entire country can be compiled into a set of individually constructive *critiques* and placed in the hands of the local radio operators with some chance of being incorporated into local program policy.

There are, today, some eighteen or twenty local groups of this nature, and because they have all enjoyed success in their undertakings to reasonable degrees, they suggest patterns for several hundred similar groups throughout the nation.

The existing organizations vary in make-up and objectives from the International Radio Council in Salt Lake City, which sponsors historical dramas for the specific purpose of educating its listeners along a particular direction, to the dynamic Cleveland Council which goes so far as to bring the commercial stations to heel for advertising excesses.

123

Some of the local groups have been fostered by the radio stations in a sincere effort to develop a meeting of minds between themselves and their listeners. Others have been set up by special interest groups among the audience as an instrument for forcing their ideas upon broadcasters.

In some cases, the organizations have a core of operating personnel with an adequate budget for day-by-day functioning, while others are merely paper structures, meeting periodically at dutch-treat luncheons to hear civic leaders and radio executives exchange compliments.

However, within those wide boundaries there can be found methods of operating feasible in any set of circumstances, and listeners who are interested in developing radio more to their use might well contemplate the formation of some such council in their own region.

The Quad-City Radio Council in Iowa suggests an excellent pattern.

This group is made up of listeners and stations in the Davenport-Rock Island-Moline area, and has been in nominal existence a little more than ten years. A year ago it was stimulated by the local radio stations, and today meets at regular intervals to undertake specific projects designed to provide better local radio service.

Although the local radio stations were responsible for the rebirth of the dormant council, the group itself is beholden to no one. The financial support, small as it is, is shared by individual members along with the radio stations and on an equal basis, and the contribution by the radio stations beyond money is no more than secretarial service.

The council is actually composed of some several hundred citizens, and all memberships are on an individual basis. There are no token memberships on the part of business firms.

The present functions of the council fall into three categories and are performed by committees. The public forum committee is responsible for the development of a series of round-table discussions on matters of local and regional interest to be heard during the fall and winter months of each year. These programs will be given the best available broadcast time by the stations, so that the citizens of the Quad-City area will have an ever-operating showcase for the discussion of community affairs.

The production committee undertakes the allocation on local radio stations of requests for air time from reputable civic and charitable groups. In this way all legitimate community undertakings will obtain broadcast time in proportion to the size of the role they play in the local scheme of things. This production committee further makes its services available to those groups to help them build radio programs of a professional nature as a means of providing better listening and better radio service to the organizations concerned.

The third function of the council commands the interest of the whole membership. It is the carrying out of this objective, stated in the council's

125

charter: "To supply all Quad-City radio stations with factual, balanced opinions of program values and station conduct."

Questionnaires are mailed to all members of the council, and each member undertakes to listen to certain program periods for a specific time, after which their ideas and opinions are correlated and turned over to the local stations for study, and, it is hoped, passed on to the national networks and advertisers in question.

A recent project grew out of the fact that one network, broadcasting in that area through one of the council's member stations, carried sixteen daytime serials in succession between the hours of one and five in the afternoon. The local station turned the problem over to its listeners, through the council, asking whether or not such a barrage of daytime serials was, possibly, too much of a good thing. Council members were asked to listen for a given week, and then suggest what they considered an ideal schedule, including, if they thought it more satisfactory, interim periods of news, music, or other non-serial fare. The station then agreed to tabulate the responses, and attempt to shuffle its block of serials in such a way as to carry out the wishes of a majority of the listeners.

Other projects will be undertaken from time to time in the field of children's programs, religious broadcasts, local sports events, etc. Slowly, the local program fare in that area will conform more perfectly to the likes of the audience itself. In the long run the station will profit by reason of a happy relationship between itself and its listeners, and the acceptance of their message by listeners who know that they have approved, not only tacitly, but actively, the program patterns, and who are in a position to make further changes if they so desire.

The National Association of Broadcasters is, of course, in complete sympathy with listener groups of this nature. Such groups provide broadcasters with a set of checks and balances that will guarantee full freedom of the air because of the guarantee to the listener against inroads on his patience and privacy.

Readers who live in cities not presently enjoying the services of a Listeners' Council are invited to correspond with the National Association of Broadcasters at 535 Fifth Avenue, New York City. This organization is always happy to send speakers to meetings of educators, public spirited citizens, and parents' groups to assist them in putting together a council of whatever pattern seems appropriate in the circumstances.

August, 1947

In the limited space of a magazine column it is impossible to describe anything more than a typical organization such as the Quad-City Council. That estimable organization is by no means the only one of its kind active today.

A complete survey of this field of activity should include lengthy studies of the work carried on by such groups as the councils in St. Louis, Kansas City,

Kokomo, Amarillo, Kalamazoo, Buffalo, Cincinnati, and Toledo, to name only a few which undertake, each year, projects peculiarly fitted to their community needs.

In Nebraska, the Omaha Radio Council has been so successful in bridging the gap between broadcasters and listeners that it is currently in the process of expansion to state-wide proportions.

In Minneapolis and St. Paul the Radio Council which was founded in 1939 has recently been called upon by the governor to aid in his three-year youth conservation program.

The Council in Des Moines is so eager to see that listeners have an understanding of the radio industry that it is sponsoring a library project, arranging for the local public libraries to have adequate shelves of literature on the subject.

The New Jersey Radio Council undertook as its particular project the education of teachers in high schools and grammar schools to uses they might make of radio in their classrooms. An exhaustive study was made of all teacher attitudes, student workshops, and the possibility of parent participation. This project served as a model for similar studies in Iowa, Utah, Minnesota, and Massachusetts.

Practically all of the councils hold annual meetings in the nature of a conference where a workshop is held to acquaint the listeners with the actual problems and functions of radio.

Most of the councils participate in the administration of the annual George Foster Peabody Awards, presented to radio stations by the University of Georgia. They organize Listening Posts and present their considered recommendations to the judges.

All this busy-ness on the part of the listeners increases immeasurably the validity of the American pattern of radio. Mr. Paul Porter, former chairman of the Federal Communications Commission, commented on the need for a constant extending and strengthening of this relationship in these words: "A greater concern with program quality by listener groups and a closer working relationship between broadcasters and representative groups are not merely desirable; they are necessary forces, it seems to me, in the democratic American system of broadcasting."

December, 1947

Program Councils

IN A RECENT ISSUE THIS COLUMN DESCRIBED THE WORK of a typical listener council, the trade designation for any quasi-formal group of radio listeners who meet periodically with radio station officials in their area for the purpose of pursuing, together, a more ideal radio service for their community. A supplementary operation, equally necessary, is a Program Production Council.

The general aims of a production council are

to pool an area's cultural, informational, and educational resources and to make them available to broadcasters under an integrated plan. A broader objective is to render to the local educational and civic groups a radio program service so that program material offered by these groups is brought to the station's listeners as professionally and dramatically as possible.

Although the need for such a service appears obvious to the average listener, the unfortunate fact remains that there are only four such councils functioning now in the United States. The oldest, and the one covering the largest area, and the one spending the greatest amount of money is the Rocky Mountain Radio Council of Denver, Colorado. The other three are: The Community Radio Council of Winston-Salem, North Carolina; The Lowell Institute Cooperative Radio Council of Boston, Massachusetts; and The Saginaw Radio Council of Saginaw, Michigan.

The latter three councils operate only on a city-wide basis, with listeners, of course, scattered as widely outside the cities as the member stations can be heard. The Rocky Mountain Radio Council, on the other hand, is regional in its scope, and serves the entire states of Wyoming and Colorado, with beneficiary listeners in the several surrounding states.

For reasons of its scope, as well as its longer history, the Rocky Mountain Council can serve as a model operation for any size area.

Although the Council's headquarters have been

in Denver from the start, Dr. Arthur Crane, president of the University of Wyoming, and chairman of the National Committee on Education by Radio, was the principal person concerned with its organization. He called a series of meetings, attended by civic and educational leaders in both states, and early in 1940 the Council was incorporated as a formal body. Mr. Robert Hudson, now with the Columbia Broadcasting System in New York, was called in to be the director of the Council, and under his guidance grade A radio facilities were made available, for the first time, to member organizations. Membership was extended to thirteen colleges and universities in the two states, and to nineteen civic and cultural groups.

Membership in the council commits an organization to an annual retainer fee which entitles each group to consultation and help in the preparation of programs which it wishes to offer to local radio stations. But it is the Council that undertakes the actual representation of the organization to the stations, securing time and overseeing the productions.

In these first seven years, though, income from fees and memberships has been insufficient to cover the extensive capital investment necessary for equipment, and foundation grants were secured to assist the group.

Naturally, no one realizes more than the people who work with these councils how the countinued reliance on grants vitiates the abilities of the members to compete in the commercial market. Only

131

when the councils develop services of a truly commercial nature inside the limited scope of their objectives will they be able to contemplate a permanency.

The present director of the Rocky Mountain Council, Mr. Allen Miller, is attempting to recast the financial structure of his group so that further grants need not be sought. To that end he has assembled a staff consisting of an associate director, a writer-producer, and two engineers. This group forms the nucleus of professional personnel whose combined salary requirements would be beyond the means of any but the largest stations in the area. The services of this group are at the disposal of local advertisers, advertising agencies, and radio stations, as well as member educational organizations. It is anticipated that they will contract for enough radio production work from year to year to put the council on a self-supporting basis. This enables advertisers to develop network-quality programs, and it further insures public service broadcasters of facilities and assistance on a professional level at charges they can afford, for the Council, being a non-profit organization, is obliged to spend any income beyond its expenses on the development of cultural programs.

In many respects, the idea of the advertisers themselves indirectly footing the bill for an adequate public service comes closest to the ideal of a strong and free commercial radio system. Radio stations, being the franchise holders for broadcast frequencies, customarily make financial contributions toward a greater public service by their gifts of broadcast time
132

to civic and community groups. They should not be asked to foot the entire bill, program and production costs, in addition to loss of revenue. The advertisers, though, are the direct beneficiaries of the American system, having available the vast audiences developed by good programming.

The council membership, likewise, should be extended to include advertisers, advertising agencies, and radio stations. It is to the advantage of all of them to have a highly professional production group at hand.

Mr. Miller does not anticipate that membership by radio stations and other commercial interests will contribute greatly to the annual budget. The principal purpose of extending membership is the insurance of a healthy participation by every pertinent organization. With a wide, active membership, it will bring to the general audience in its area not only more finely finished commercial programs, but expertly tailored educational and informational programs. Annual campaigns by such groups as the Community Chest, Red Cross, and other welfare agencies will be fitted into over-all yearly patterns. If disasters occur, a mechanism is already available for harnessing the area's radio facilities.

From a longer view, the council provides a training ground for radio personnel. Too frequently in the past young people who might have developed program material of genuine value have found no place where they might be trained.

The experience of the four councils indicates

that an active and valuable organization can be operated on an annual budget as low as Winston-Salem's $2,000, or on as lavish a scale as is carried out in Denver for $32,000.

October, 1947

An Academy Proposal

ONE SUBJECT YOU WILL NEVER HEAR DISCUSSED AMONG the prosperous commercial radio practitioners is the Art of Radio. And you will range widely among the teachers, theoreticians, and critics without hearing a sensible and responsible discussion of the Business of Broadcasting.

There is, unfortunately, a wide schism between those two powerful and at present antagonistic segments of the industry. Until that breach is healed, the broadcasters will resist even the most constructive of outside criticism, and the critics will continue to abhor commercialism in general, which amounts to a rejection not only of specific programs, but of the entire American system. In no other field of entertainment can there be found such vigorous and dissentious dogmatism.

All of which is a preamble to the statement that now that it has passed into the second quarter-century of its existence, radio most certainly needs, and patently merits, a repository for whatever lasting values it has created for itself. Such a perpetuation is neces-

134

sary if present suicidal business practices are ever to be weeded out and if the left-bankishness of its artisans is to be directed to concrete attainments. An institute is suggested, a permanent body whose function might best be defined by the name Academy of Radio Arts and Sciences.

The idea of an Academy is not new. Norman Corwin devoted considerable time and effort to the establishment of such a body in 1944 and 1945. His plans, though, went awry when he solicited the aid of the National Association of Broadcasters. That active and worthy trade organization felt that the functions of an Academy could best be undertaken by itself and that the establishment of another body, no matter how august, would only complicate the situation.

That thesis rests on a fundamental fallacy. The objectives of a trade organization should be the daily bulwarking of business against the ebbing and flowing tides of circumstance, opinion, and affairs. The executives of the NAB would be defeating their own ends were they to divide their attention between the eternal and temporal. On the other hand, the functions of an Academy would be hindered were it too closely concerned with the day-by-day course of events in the broadcasting field.

Such an Academy should not concern itself with matters of trade regulation, legislation, and transient public relations. An Academy should provide, instead, a meeting place for thinking men and women whose interest in radio is speculative rather than

135

practical. Social scientists, editors, writers, philosophers, psychologists, statesmen—there are many of them in this country who occupy themselves from time to time with the contemplation of the broader psychological, sociological, and literary implications of radio.

Today, as matters stand, there is no way for the results of the training and thinking of these men to be channelized into the industry where good use might be made of their efforts. True, much of their work is too abstract to have any practical application at a given moment, but its compilation into a permanent set of reports and integrated documentation would provide commercial radio men of the future with more accurate charts for the navigation of the shoals of public manners, morals, and tastes.

Considerable material is finding publication today which is pertinent to long range thinking and planning, but it is appearing in obscure quarterlies and specialized learned journals. There is, in radio, no medium where the businessman and the philosopher can meet on common ground and where the scientist and the artist can exchange views and conclusions. Such a journal, besides serving as a clearing house for important papers on interesting new facets of the industry, would be a useful forum for discussion on the problem of training the broadcasters of tomorrow.

Each year finds a greater number of schools and universities instituting courses in radio-broadcasting. From a course in radio acting, introduced into the curriculum of their speech departments a decade ago, many colleges have now expanded to full four-year courses which attempt to teach the student something about every phase of the broadcasting industry. In many cases, the university owns a radio station which even competes to a modest degree with commercial stations in its area.

With all due respect to the integrity and the intentions of the professors of broadcasting in these courses, it must be said that they are so far removed from the actualities of the business that they teach little of practical value. Yet in greater and greater numbers the graduates of these courses are finding their way into the industry. Would there not be great investment value in organizing a channel through which today's broadcasters could help direct the training of those who will follow after them? An Academy engaging the efforts of both the broadcasters and the scholar would have the respect of students as well as advertisers, and would provide neophytes of radio with guidance, wisdom, and an operating philosophy—to say nothing of a set of standards of teaching.

Among the United Nations—to turn to another phase of the problem—the United States speaks with a vigorous voice. The programs being beamed to the rest of the world by the International Broadcasting Division of the Department of State are, in many cases, the actual implements of our foreign policy. They attempt to explain to the average listener overseas, in dramatic radio terms, the reasons behind the news, the background of events, and the goals toward which we are working. And we are not alone in this field. The competition for listener attention is as vigorous in the international field as in any city in the country entered by the four networks. There are fifty-five nations engaged in this battle for listeners.

In this situation, the entire industry is at stake. The merit of the American system of radio is under scrutiny by the rest of the world, and yet there exists no formal liaison through which the best talents in the country can be placed at the service of the nation. A committee of an Academy, embracing the efforts not only of broadcasters, but of professionals in the field of international relations, could do much toward the proper accomplishment of the obvious objectives in this short-wave operation.

And so it goes—publications, studies, and giving of prizes, there is no area of endeavor within the field of broadcasting which could not benefit greatly by the establishment of an academy-like body to harness the know-how of commercial radio with the know-what of competent observers and scientists.

And yet the task is for the industry, not for the scholars. Scholasticism is a means, not an end. The end is the perpetuation of the American system as we know it and enjoy it in our homes, listening. The means should be systematic and sober self-analysis with the object of perpetuating that which is good, and thinning out obsolete attitudes which stem from too fragile a knowledge of the Thing in Itself. It

would be useless for the theoreticians to attempt to
organize such an undertaking, no matter how acutely
conscious they are of the need for it. The practical
workers, the broadcasters, will know how to shape it
to their purposes once the project is assured.

March, 1947

6 • The Bookshelf

Norman Corwin

> *Thirteen by Corwin.* Radio plays by Nor-
> man Corwin. New York; Henry Holt & Co.
> 1942. 338 pp. $2.75.

At the age of thirty-one, Norman Corwin is an
old man in radio. The average age for innovation in
this field seems to be twenty-fivish—witness Orson
Welles, John Latouche, Irving Reiss, and Arch Oboler. Youthfulness is abundant in radio because of
the greater opportunities offered for experiment, and
because of the absence of maturity as a criterion.

Reading this collection of thirteen of Corwin's
radio plays, though, the reader will look in vain for
the hallmarks of slow artistic development—the sober
introspection, the long digested thoughts of others.
Corwin did not develop more slowly than the others;
he merely got a later start in radio. Born and brought
up in the vicinity of Boston, he went into newspaper

6 · THE BOOKSHELF

work after graduating from high school. Some ad-
mirers call him a better writer than director, and
others a better director than writer; but he calls himself a better journalist than either. Indeed, a close
examination of all his plays reveals that his best and
most moving efforts have been those built on the documentary, or reportorial, structure.

His early newspaper career took him to Springfield, Massachusetts, where he handled sports and
sundry special events. At heart a lover of poetry,
and a dabbler in rhyme himself, he became intrigued
by the possibilities of radio as a better vehicle for
poetry than the printed page, and, shortly after com-
ing to Springfield, made his debut on one of the local
stations in a program called "Rhymes and Cadences,"
which was an attempt to test standard poetical works
against musical patterns and to find new ways to
heighten the emotional effect of verse on the listener.

In 1937, he came to New York and took a job
in the publicity department of a large movie company. At that sterile time there was only one radio
station in New York available for a continuation of
his literary adventures—WQXR, owned by Mr. John
V. L. Hogan, himself an experimenter in methods of
transmitting music, who was gaining fame with a
station catering to the intelligentsia. Corwin's forays into this field of mobile poetry fitted nicely into
the station's program policy, and so, during the winter of 1937 and the spring of 1938, he carried on with
much the same sort of program he had used in
Springfield, calling his show "Poetic License." In

141

this feature he drew heavily upon the modern American poets who seemed to lend themselves more readily to dramadaption, to coin a word, filling in from time to time with works of his own.

Always, he was less interested in content than in the presentation. A new way to pour old wine has been the object of his constant search, and through that search he has probably contributed as much as any editor or critic to the popular enjoyment of serious poetry.

He took verse from the printed page where it could be appreciated by only the most literate, and gave it voice, sound effects, music, dialect—in short, all the dramatic effects of true theater. Such effects were imposed upon works like *Spoon River Anthology* and *Leaves of Grass* with surprisingly happy results from both a critical and entertainment point of view.

Despite all this, he was still confined to a small weekly feature on a small local station. His brother, Emil Corwin, whom Norman describes as his most consistent critic and mentor, was then working in the publicity department of NBC. In his efforts to find a place for Norman in network radio, brother Emil finally persuaded the powers-that-be that Norman's little feature would make an interesting act in a then-famous variety show—"The Magic Key of RCA," a weekly hour program done by the Radio Corporation of America. Norman's appearance on that program, although called by *Variety* "something that idea-hungry networks could use," went unno-

142

ticed by the program heads of NBC.

However, Mr. William Lewis, program vice-president of the Columbia Broadcasting System, unlike the NBC officials, was aware of the trend toward more articulate radio. He noticed Corwin and offered him a job as a director at CBS. After a few months, his first big series went on the air. This program, called "Words Without Music," was an adaptation of his earlier efforts on a grander scale. He was given a half hour each Sunday afternoon, money to hire a cast of actors, and a budget to encourage writers to submit material.

The success of this first series and the subsequent awakening of interest in the more literary uses of radio led, a year later, to another, and more ambitious series—"The Pursuit of Happiness." This series was one of the very first in radio given over to cementing morale behind the birthing defense effort. Started in 1940, it began to sing the American song at a time when this country was in the deepest trough of isolationism. On that show John Latouche's "Ballad for Americans" was given its first national hearing, and that fine piece of patriotic balladry rather well defined the mood of the entire series.

By now, Corwin had become a commodity. He lectured. He wrote poems for *Esquire*. An enthusiastic play producer gave him an advance on an unwritten play. And he had several movie offers. After a short trip to Hollywood where he did the screen play for Elmer Rice's *Two on an Island,* he came back East to embark on his largest assignment—a series

143

of twenty-six plays in one full series, titled, simply enough, "Twenty-six by Corwin."

The twenty-six plays were over in the early fall of 1941. By then we were at war, emotionally if not actually, and Archibald MacLeish, Pulitzer Prize poet and Librarian of Congress, was mobilizing the nation's poets and playwrights into a propaganda machine. Corwin, poet, radio dramatist, and "Dean" of radio writers, fitted the need perfectly, and to him was entrusted the task of putting on the notable "Bill of Rights" broadcast. In that program the free use of verse and effect, always Corwin's strong point, proved once and for all that radio, if given to such people as he, without qualifications, could outshine any other form of inspirational pageant.

Carl Van Doren says, in his preface to this collection of radio plays, that to the author goes the credit not only for seeing what might be done with the radio script as an art form, but also for doing it as a whole series of plays, poetic or humorous, exhibiting the full range of his art.

That's a rather large order, and I'm sure Corwin himself would be among the first to disclaim that rather awesome distinction. Orson Welles, Arch Oboler, and Irving Reiss all predated Corwin by two or three years. True, not all of them were poets, but neither is Corwin a Shakespearian actor like Welles. But all of them were busily seeing what might be done with the radio script as an art form. Possibly Corwin's greatest distinction over the others is that he was awarded, early in 1942, at the Annual Adver-

144

tising Awards dinner in New York, the Edward Bok memorial medal for being ". . . the individual who by contemportry service has added to the knowledge or technique of radio advertising." This award made a keen distinction between this one writer and his colleagues by designating him as having given special service to the advance of radio as an *advertising* medium. In effect that award was not so much a gesture to Corwin himself as an acceptance at long last by the realists that radio itself has something more to offer the mature mind and the serious thinker.

This collection of thirteen plays does not represent all of the author's finest radio drama, nor all of his lightest and most easily assimilated pieces, but rather a sampling from his whole four years in big-time radio. They indicate a full and worthwhile literature from a period when the average advertiser or radio professional would tell you that "art" had no place in radio. When the ordinary expert wrote "down" to the people, Corwin dabbled in blank verse and choral effects. He has never been over-civilized, nor does he pretend to believe in art for art's sake, but rather he has been fighting in defense of the principle that radio can tell a stronger story than the one of "Aunt Minnie's broken back, burning house, blind daughter, and thieving husband, and soap." He also believes that radio can and should use stronger and more complicated symbols than are used in the nursery. The mind of the average listener may be that of the twelve-year-old child, as radio experts had held in defense of their own failure to

145

provide more mature fare, but Corwin assumes that a mind of any age can be moved and attracted by the same literary devices that have engaged and motivated the average minds over centuries through plays, religious ceremonies, political pageants, and occasional festivals, and with that assumption, he has steadily worked at infusing radio with the ideas, the lofty prose, the illumined dialogue, the fine verse of sturdier dramatists of braver days.

To Norman Corwin, then, not the credit for first seeing what radio could do as an art form, but rather for so patiently nourishing it that other people could see the same thing.

As poetry to be judged by more competent critics Corwin's works might lack maturity, as indeed any work by a man of his years might. And as one listens to his programs week after week one is conscious of faltering dramaturgy here and there. But that is the fault of the medium rather than of the man. The playwriting in his half year series "Twenty-Six" was equal in volume to six full-length plays, a record for fertility that has rarely been matched. He did not do it as a virtuosity, but rather because a radio series has to be done all at once, or not at all.

Van Doren likens him to Marlowe, but the reference appears to be chronological rather than stylistic —both seem to stand at the doorway to their field. rather than in the center. And it may well be true that other writers will come along who will say nobler things better than Corwin, because radio is still a young art, and its practitioners are still not free from wonderment at the flexibility and the elasticity of the medium. Not until another generation comes along which will not remember the chaotic, inarticulate adolescence of radio will writers be able to work in radio with a complete absence of self-consciousness about the tools of their craft. When writers can write and directors direct without wondering "how it would sound" with this trick or that, radio will produce men of letters whose reputations will be as sure as those of novelists, historians, or biographers, poets or playwrights.

February, 1942

Max Wylie

Best Broadcasts of 1939-40. Selected and Edited by Max Wylie. New York: Whittlesey House. 1940. 368pp. $3.00.

IN AN ATTEMPT TO DO FOR RADIO WHAT BURNS MANtle has been doing for the theater and Edward J. O'Brien for the short story, Max Wylie, head of the script division of the Columbia Broadcasting System, has brought out his second annual anthology of the Best Broadcasts. The word "best" is a dangerous choice in any event, and in the field of radio it would seem to cast a fatal shadow of conjecture over the entire endeavor. Best? Best for what purpose? Best according to what standards?

Apparently Mr. Wylie has many methods of

147

choice. There is, for instance, a script by Arch Obo-ler—"This Lonely Heart," which was written to *accompany* certain Tschaikovsky music, and which, in script form, can be appreciated only by those most expert radio men with a knowledge of music. Then, in the same category, there is a monologue by W. H. Auden, which reads pleasantly enough, but would not live through its translation into broadcast. The question arises, what in a radio show is good—the literary finery in the background, or the emotional impact of the total sound of it?

In the field of comedy and variety, the anthologist is on surer ground, because he embraces, in his choices, all possibilities. Jack Benny, Fred Allen, Burns and Allen, Bob Hope, and the Aldrich family are all given equal billing in this field. He's right. No matter what standards are applied, one of these shows is sure to be on top. However, in the field of radio education, his judgment is open to question. He neglects several powerful and evocative ventures which have been presented in this last year.

Then, there are several speeches, newscasts, and sports broadcasts which provoke interesting conjecture about how they may have sounded when they were timely and of immediate interest. Here again, what part of radio has inherent literary value, and what part depends upon the occasion?

The book is interesting to anyone in the trade who might wonder what Mr. Wylie thinks are "good programs." Beyond that, its lack of pattern deadens its impact. The most valuable portion of the book

is the preface, in which Mr. Wylie discusses reasons
for the absence of accurate critical standards for radio
programs.

October, 1940

Arch Oboler

Fourteen Radio Plays. By Arch Oboler.
New York: Random House. 1940. 257pp.
$2.00.

RADIO HAS COME OF AGE. IN NOVEMBER, 1940, DO-
mestic broadcasting passed its twentieth anniversary.
A coincidental proof of this fact is this publication
of a collection of radio plays by Mr. Arch Oboler—
the first collection of works by a single radio writer
ever to appear. Oboler, mind you, is no famous poet,
novelist, or playwright who has merely turned to
radio—he has written only for broadcast, and his
prestige as a writer is in that one field only. With this
publication radio is at last formally, and deservingly,
recognized as a branch of Letters.

During the childhood of radio, its literature was
not taken seriously. Bad novels and worse plays were
adapted for microphone presentation, but original
works were tolerated rather than appreciated. In the
absence of criteria, the fact of a story's having been
published in book form, or in a magazine, or having
had a stage production appeared to testify to its excellence for radio listening. As for authors, a similar
condition was, and still is, true: a recognized author

149

in any field is better than a radio writer. Why? Because the recognized author can point to published works as proof of his talents, while the radio writer has no tangible proof. Again, there are no critical standards.

Radio is a new form. Being a stimulus simply and directly to the ear, it is most like music in its impact, swifter and stronger than the plastic arts or the visual theater in its appeal to the senses, and it depends first and primarily on the words—not upon the scene, nor the color, nor the movement, but only the words. Radio writers like Oboler, like Norman Corwin, John Latouche, and Irving Reiss are sensitive to this knowledge, and work simply with the word —the bare, naked word and its meaning. Because of this fact about radio, there will be wiser prophets, greater story tellers, and finer poets among us than at present, but not until the public accepts radio writers for their own worth rather than for the glory reflected from their accomplishments in other fields. This acceptance will come, slowly perhaps, but certainly, for radio is now an adult instrument, standing side by side with the theater, the motion picture, the novel, the poem, and the pamphlet. The publication of this first volume of radio plays is tangible proof of this adulthood, and evidence that the acceptance of it has begun.

December, 1940

Sherman Dryer

Radio In Wartime. By Sherman Dryer.
New York: Greenburg. 1942. 384pp. $3.00.

FOR THE WRITER WHO IS LEANING TOWARD RADIO, THE editor attempting to broaden his knowledge of media, the scholar or educator surveying methods for increasing the force of his ideas, and especially for the reader who wants to widen his acquaintance with the methods by which the war is being fought, this collection of essays on radio's possibilities in wartime will be a useful and long-awaited addition.

Impresario of the famous University of Chicago Round Table, Mr. Dryer's intimate knowledge of how radio functions in that delicate situation—the open forum or the round table—enables him to draw and support many suspected, but never demonstrated, conclusions concerning radio as an instrument for creating opinions and attitudes. And, realizing that no one set of conclusions can ever be inviolate, he has called on such radio-wise propagandists, public relations experts, and writers as Dr. Harold D. Lasswell, Max Lerner, Arch Oboler, and Edward L. Bernays to offer comments out of their own experiences on the different subjects the book discusses.

Although the point of departure of the book is the open forum, a somewhat rare form of radio program, the truth about any form of radio is true about all forms. Mr. Dryer discusses the important prob-